HARDY'S
Poetic Drama and the Theatre

By the same author

Tess In The Theatre

[The two dramatizations of *Tess of the D'Urbervilles* by
Thomas Hardy and one by Lorimer Stoddard edited, with
an introduction by Marguerite Roberts, Ph.D.] Copyright,
Canada, 1950, by University of Toronto Press and printed
in Canada.
London: Geoffrey Cumberlege, Oxford University Press.

HARDY'S

Poetic Drama and the Theatre

The Dynasts

and

The Famous Tragedy of the Queen of Cornwall

Marguerite Roberts

"Aristotle's opinion still holds; the greatest poetry remains dramatic and epic." Donald A. Stauffer

Pageant Press, Inc.
New York

Library of Congress Catalog Card Number: 65-22482

FIRST EDITION

Published by Pageant Press, Inc.
101 Fifth Avenue, New York, N. Y. 10003

Manufactured in the United States of America

For
Alice Roberts Barrett
and
Ralph R. Roberts

"*The Dynasts* (1902-1908) is now probably more read than any of the novels; it is in some sense the product less of those years than of a lifetime."

J. W. M.

Order of Proceedings at the unveiling of the Memorial Statue of Thomas Hardy O.M. Dorchester, September 2, 1931.

"It seems to me that if we are to have a poetic drama, it is more likely to come from poets learning to write plays than from skilful prose dramatists learning to write poetry."

T. S. Eliot, *Poetry and Drama,* the first Theodore Spencer Memorial lecture.

Acknowledgments

The material for this study came primarily from Max Gate, as did that for the book, *Tess and the Theatre*, and the larger work *Hardy and the Theatre*. Since Mrs. Hardy realized that Hardy was not thought of as a dramatist and felt that Hardy's relationship with the theatrical world was not sufficiently recognized, she graciously gave me every facility for exploring this field. At Max Gate, she made available to me Hardy's correspondence with Granville Barker concerning *The Dynasts* in 1914 at the Kingsway Theatre, and that with Maurice Colbourne and Charles Morgan concerning the production at Oxford in 1920. My visits to Mrs. Hardy at Adelphi Terrace in London as well as Max Gate in Dorchester were memorable occasions and afforded unforgettable associations.

Miss Irene Cooper Willis and Lloyd Banks of London as trustees of the Hardy copyright have given me permission to use the unpublished Hardy material, as have Macmillan and Company given permission for the published. In London shortly after the second World War in her chambers in Lincoln's Inn, Miss Cooper Willis took down from her book-shelves Granville Barker's "marked copy" of *The Dynasts* and entrusted it to me. This is the copy which Granville Barker referred to in his letter to

Hardy when he first broached the subject of producing *The Dynasts* in London. In a hurricane on a trans-Atlantic flight in which the plane endured unbelievable buffeting, the responsibility of this "marked copy" proved a cause for concern from Iceland to Nova Scotia.

Maurice Colbourne and Charles Morgan have given permission for their letters to Hardy to be included in this study. My indebtedness to Maurice Colbourne goes back to the time of his theatrical tour of Canada during the second World War with a troupe of British actors. At that time, he kindly answered many of my questions about the Oxford production. Later, in England, he let me peruse the scrapbooks of the O.U.D.S. and lent me his copy of the Granville Barker script as directed by A. E. Drinkwater in London and Oxford. Colonel C. Archer has kindly given me permission to use the letters of his brother, William Archer. Lady Keeble, the first Mrs. Granville Barker, wrote me about the script used at the Kingsway Theatre. Mr. Allan Wade, a member of Granville Barker's cast wrote me about the production, and Mr. Carl J. Weber has given me access to his own extensive Hardy material as well as the Colby College Collection.

At Gordon Villa Mr. T. H. Tilley, former mayor of Dorchester and stage manager of the Hardy Players, shared his memories of the seventy-two performances of fourteen different Hardy plays. To him I am indebted for the scripts of *The Wessex Scenes from The Dynasts* and *The Famous Tragedy of the Queen of Cornwall* as produced by the Hardy Players in Dorchester and London. And in the busy week preceding the opening of the Bath Festival in 1935, Mr. Rutland Boughton took time during a rehearsal of his music-drama, *The Ever Young,* at the Bath Pavilion to tell me how he composed and produced his opera, *The Queen of Cornwall.*

My use of the Widener Library and the Harvard Theatre Collection in particular while working on this subject has been continuous; and at the Houghton Library of Harvard I have found some new material from recent accessions which has been incorporated in these pages. I gratefully acknowledge permission of the Harvard College Library to incorporate the manuscript of Helen Huntington Granville Barker. At the time of the first handling of this material on *Hardy and the Theatre* as part of a Radcliffe requirement, I shall always be grateful for the invaluable advice and encouragement of the late Professor Theodore Spencer of Harvard. For the time and opportunity to rewrite some portions pertaining to the poetic drama, I am indebted to President George M. Modlin and the trustees of the University of Richmond for sabbatical leave. For making all the facilities of Harvard and Radcliffe available to me as a Research Fellow, I am grateful to President Mary L. Bunting and the Radcliffe Graduate Council. Finally, I wish to acknowledge assistance from the Research Committee of the University of Richmond for a grant from the Seay Education Fund to help make this volume possible.

M. R.

January 1, 1965
Richmond, Virginia

CONTENTS

CONTENTS

HARDY'S
Poetic Drama and the Theatre

Hardy's Interest in the Theatre

There are many indications of Hardy's early attraction to the stage. His reading of drama, his attendance of plays, and his correspondence with people of the theatre are among them. But perhaps we should not overlook the fact that as a small boy Hardy was no exception to Archer's dictum, "The child, whether savage or civilized, is a born actor," [1] or Aristotle's "the instinct of imitation is implanted in man from childhood." [2] Mrs. Hardy relates several little incidents [3] illustrating the truth of these statements. Hardy and his mother, for example, would disguise themselves in fantastic garb with cabbage-nets over their faces and walk across the heath to Puddletown to surprise his amazed aunt. She also says that at the age of seven, Hardy (probably imitating some of the demonstrations he saw during the Corn Law Agitation) would dip his wooden sword in the blood of a newly killed pig and brandish it exclaiming, "Free trade or Blood." Mr. Weber attributes the imitation of sheep to Hardy and records that Hardy remembered to the end of his life looking up and seeing the astonishment of the sheep standing around watching him crawling on all fours pretending to eat grass. [4] But perhaps the best early example of Hardy's dramatic instinct is found in his dramatization of the church services. We might have felt ourselves in the presence of vital realistic drama, if we could have seen him wrapped in a tablecloth, standing on a chair, fervently reading the morning prayer to his cousin and grandmother on wet Sunday mornings. His service caused his hearers to say he would be a parson, "being obviously no good for any practical pursuit." [5]

In the thatch-covered cottage at the edge of Egdon Heath, Hardy had opportunities for developing his innate dramatic sense. Mr. Brennecke presents a charming idyll:

> In the rambling, comfortable Hardy House, the village "Quire" assembled every week to rehearse their dance tunes, rounds, and carols; in this house also the neighborly folk gathered to celebrate the recurring rural festivals; here, before the blazing hearth, they presented their traditional lyric-dramatic-choreographic bits, like the delightful *O Jan! O Jan! O Jan!* the memory of which was to endure for at least four score years.[6]

It is evident from Mrs. Hardy's statement concerning the choir in *Under the Greenwood Tree* that Hardy did not remember the rehearsals of the choir. "Thomas Hardy the Third invented the personages, incidents, manners, etc., never having seen the choir as such, they ending their office when he was about a year old." [7] If, however, Hardy did not know the choir, he at least knew the festivals with their music and dance and folk lore, the basis of his dramas of Wessex. The mummers cast their spell upon him.

Mr. Roger S. Loomis, who modernized *The Play of St. George,* says:

2

Mr. Thomas Hardy has confessed that one of the yearnings of his youth was to fill the comic role of the Doctor. But his parents were afraid that trudging down muddy lanes and across frosty heaths might reduce young Thomas to a state where all the virtues of his sovereign remedy would be of no avail; and he remained perforce a mere spectator.[8]

It is delightful to think of Hardy at the age of four playing on an accordion, his father's gift on his birthday with the date, 1844, inscribed. He came from a family of musicians. His grandfather gave thirty-five years to the "Mellstock Quire" as one of the ecclesiastical bandsmen, who would "blare and scrape" the Psalms on Sunday but like Grandfather William would tune his viol at a party "as irreligiously as could be desired." Thomas Hardy was very sensitive to melody though he was not a skilled musician. He was, according to Mrs. Hardy:

of an ecstatic temperament, extraordinarily sensitive to music, and among the endless jigs, hornpipes, reels, waltzes, and country dances that his father played in the evening in his early married years, and to which the boy danced a *pas seul* in the middle of the room, there were three or four that always moved the child to tears, though he strenuously tried to hide them. Among these airs (though he did not know their names at the time) were, by the way, "Enrico" (popular in the Regency), "The Fairy Dance," "Miss Macleod of Ayr" (an old Scotch tune to which Burns may have danced), and a melody named "My Fancy Lad" or "Johnny's gone to sea." This peculiarity in himself troubled

3

the mind of "Tommy" as he was called, and set him wondering at a phenomenon to which he ventured not confess. He used to say in later life that, like Calantha in Ford's *Broken Heart,* he danced on at these times to conceal his weeping.[9]

His mother also contributed to this dramatic background. She was an omnivorous reader, and she sang the sacred and secular songs of the period. She had an extraordinary store of local ballads from which Hardy learned the traditional drama of Dorset. With such a background it is natural that young Hardy should have been interested in folk drama. His suggestion in the last paragraph to the preface of *The Dynasts* "of the monotonic delivery of speeches, with dreamy, conventional gestures, something in the manner traditionally maintained by the old Christmas mummers" [10] springs from this love of Wessex lore. His early surroundings account for his use of homely dramatic incidents and for the justification of the correspondents in the heyday of the Hardy Players in expecting Hardy to bring in country songs and dances.

Hardy knew the drama also from his reading. He was well acquainted with the drama of the Greeks and the Elizabethans. Along with the romances of Dumas *père* he was reading Shakespeare critically at the age of twelve. He confessed that he did not think much of *Hamlet* "because the ghost did not play his part up to the end as he ought to have done." [11] When he was a student of architecture in London he saw Charles Kean and his wife in Shakespearean plays at the Princess. He went to the theatre to study Shakespeare for the poetry [12] and the drama, for he told Charles Morgan that he would sit in the front

4

row with the text in hand and "follow the dialogue by the stage light." [13]

Hardy studied Greek tragedy, which he admired all his life. Although advised to devote himself to the study of architecture rather than read *Agamemnon* and *Oedipus* in the original, he obtained a substantial knowledge of the works of Aeschylus and Sophocles. Their influence is felt throughout his work. "That Greek conception entered deeply into Hardy's thought would be apparent through the rhythm and burden of his writings." [14] Aeschylus and Sophocles were his models especially for *The Return of the Native* and *The Dynasts,* in the last of which he was especially close to the epic ideal where he brooded on questions of destiny and *Immanent Will.* Mr. Hedgcock says Hardy's work shows the combination of the Elizabethan with the Greek influence. *"Émule moderne des tragiques grecs et des dramaturges anglais de l'époque elizabethenne, il cherche à présenter les vieux problèmes enrichis de vérités nouvelles."* [15]

In addition to reading Shakespeare, Aeschylus, and Sophocles, Hardy as a young man in London often went to the theatre. Catholic in his taste, he attended opera, music halls, and ballets. He viewed tragedy, comedy, and melodrama. He saw plays and operas in Norwegian, French, Italian, as well as English.

He heard the foreign operas of Rossini, Donizetti, Verdi, Meyerbeer, and Bellini in vogue in the 'sixties and thus became familiar with such singers as Tietjens, Nilsson, Patti, Guiglini, and Parepa. He also attended the performances of the English Opera Company where he heard the music of Balfe, Wallace and others.[16] In June, 1873, he saw French plays; in the 'eighties he attended French ballets as well as French plays in London.

5

In Dorchester, he went to see circuses and strolling play-ers. In 1890, he saw Irving in *The Bells;* in 1891, Kotze-bue's *The Stranger* and Elizabeth Robins in *Hedda Gabler;* in 1893 *Hedda Gabler* again, *Rosmerholm,* and the *Master Builder,* as well as performances by Ada Rehan and Eleanora Duse. In 1895, he saw Forbes Robertson and Mrs. Patrick Campbell in *Romeo and Juliet.* There is more evidence of Hardy's attending the theatre in the 'nineties in a series of four letters in the Harvard Theatre Collection. Hardy sent a note to Augustin Daly, in 1893: "My best thanks for the charming scene to which we were introduced last night, and for the fine piece of acting which graced it. Commendation in detail is superfluous, this having been bestowed by better pens than mine."

Again on July 3, 1893, he wrote Daly: "I am tempted to avail myself of the kind suggestion in your note, by asking if there are 2 places to be had for the matinee next Saturday, a friend of high critical acumen and taste, whom I am anxious should be favorably impressed by your company, could go with me that afternoon."

Two years later Daly must have invited Hardy another time as his guest to the theatre, for Hardy wrote, July 8, 1895: "We could come tomorrow, Tuesday, to the play —or Wednesday, if the house is full for Tuesday." And again on July 11, 1895, Hardy said: "Many thanks for the box— We enjoyed the play much." These letters are significant of Hardy's friendly relation with at least one producer at the time he had finished *The Three Way-farers* (1893), and the dramatization of *Tess* (1895).

Hardy continued to enjoy Greek drama till the end of his life. In January, 1912, he saw *Oedipus* at Covent Garden. Three times he entertained the Balliol Players, undergraduates of Oxford, when they came to Max Gate to give their performances on the lawn. On July 1, 1924, they gave *The Oresteia* as *The Curse of the House of Atreus;* on June 29, 1926, *Hippolytus* of Euripides; and about six months before his death, July 6, 1927, *Iphigenia in Aulis.*

The Harley Granville Barkers were present at two of the productions by the Oxford undergraduates. Helen Huntington Granville Barker wrote an unpublished account of these productions:

> The Balliol Players from Oxford gave three performances in the tiny garden of Max Gate. Its high hedges took the place of wings, woodwork, and background. The lawn and trees and sky were there instead of a painted canvas scene. In the foreground looking, we all said,—so suitable and so Greek—almost—was Hardy's plaster urn—I forget its history—the sole ornament of the garden. On one occasion was Euripedes' *Hippolytus.* Some of the young men did look Greek—as English lads often do—and they had beautiful voices, but their wigs suggested the Bar more than Attikos—huge hoods of wool rather than hair. The young man chosen for Phedre had a hairy chest, and a deep bass voice.
>
> But none of these incongruities and absurdities troubled T.H. He sat a little apart from the rest of the audience of six—the *Euripedes* text, with the translation, on his knee, following the speeches of the actors. Birds and butterflies flew about a small portable structure that represented in turn, temple, palace, or warriors' tent. The colour in the sky deepened as the sun grew lower, rooks in the trees outshrilled the actors.
>
> On one occasion the play was *Orestes*—and

7

"Puffin" Asquith appeared first as Clytemnestra, then as Orestes' old nurse and then as the leading Fury—his resemblance to his mother more noticeable in each now rôle.

One never knew what T.H. thought of the acting generally. He was always craftily shrewd when it came to expressing opinions on contemporary effort of any kind. He didn't, of course, want to be quoted, but, even more, he didn't want to be wrong. When he approved it was seldom more than joining in a choir of general approval. His own apprehension of life and death and humanity was that of genius, but when it came to projecting himself into the conceptions of another creator or critic he was either tired or feeble.[17]

Hardy was connected with the theatre through his friends. Among the playwrights whom he entertained at Max Gate were Sir James Barrie, Bernard Shaw, John Galsworthy, Henry Arthur Jones, as well as Harley Granville Barker. Among dramatic critics he had many friends including Sir Edmund Gosse, William Archer, J. T. Grein, Max Beerbohm and Charles Morgan. His correspondence with actors, actresses, managers, and operatic composers was large. Some of Hardy's friends of the theatrical world sought him at Max Gate, others invited him to London. Mrs. Hardy records that he called on Irving in his dressing room after his performance in *Richard III,* that he supped with Mrs. Patrick Campbell and Forbes Robertson at Will's after their performance in *Romeo and Juliet.* Hardy's connection with the theatre increased throughout his life. He brushed aside the inquiries of the theatrical world for his work in England in the 'nineties but welcomed them after his work on *The Dynasts* was done in 1908. He even took an active interest in his later years in having his work staged by Dorchester players, the Oxford University Dramatic Society, and by some professional managers.

Hardy considered preparing himself for a playwright before he was a novelist. In the early part of 1867, he investigated the stage with that in view. Mrs. Hardy explains his intention at that time:

> It should be mentioned that several months before leaving London he had formed the idea of writing plays in blank verse—and planned to try the stage as a supernumerary for six or twelve months, to acquire technical skill in their construction—going so far as to make use of an introduction to Mark Lemon, the then editor of *Punch,* and an ardent amateur-actor, for his opinion on the point. Nothing, however, came of the idea beyond the call on the genial editor, and on Mr. Coe, the stage-manager at the Haymarket under Buckstone's lesseeship, with whom he had a conversation. The former rather damped the young man's ardour by reminding him that the elder Mathews had said that he would not let a dog of his go on the stage, and that he himself, much as he personally liked the art of acting, would rather see a daughter in her grave than on the boards of a theatre. In fact almost the first moment of his sight of stage realities disinclined him to push further in that direction; and his only actual contact with the stage at this time was his appearance at Covent Garden as a nondescript in the pantomime of "The Forty Thieves," and in a representation of the Oxford and Cambridge boat-

9

race—this having come about through the accident of the smith who did the ironwork for the pantomime being the man who executed some of Blomfield's designs for the church metal-work, and who made crucifixes and harlequin-traps with equal imperturbability. More than forty years were to elapse before Hardy trod the same boards again —this time at the rehearsals of the Italian Opera by Baron Frederic d'Erlanger, founded on *Tess of the D'Urbervilles.*[18]

In addition to Hardy's interest in folk drama and the professional theatre, we are aware of an everpresent dramatic element in his work. His whole theory of writing consisted in making tales unusual enough to stop wedding guests, as he wrote in his diary on February 23, 1893:

> A story must be exceptional enough to justify its telling. We tale-tellers are all Ancient Mariners, and none of us is warranted stopping Wedding Guests . . . unless he has something more unusual to relate than the ordinary experience of the average man and woman. The whole secret of fiction and the drama—in the constructional part—lies in the adjustment of things unusual to things eternal and universal.[19]

Hardy's stories abound in unusual objective action— dramatic and sometimes melodramatic. Since plot was of paramount importance to him, his stories are never static. Sometimes they are most powerful. Often they contain dramatic or spectacular scenes. One needs to cite merely the feat of showmanship in the hollow amid the ferns in *Far from the Madding Crowd,* where Sergeant Troy carves out the figure of Bathsheba; the ironical situation in *A Pair of Blue Eyes* where the two lovers, Smith and Knight, hasten to propose to Elfreda but find they have traveled on the same train with her corpse; the sale of the wife at the beginning of *The Mayor of Casterbridge;* Mrs. Yeobright's walk across the heath in *The Return of the Native;* the murder of Alec in *Tess of the d'Urbervilles;* or the ghastly death of the children in *Jude the Obscure.* Scenes such as these have led me to say—as Pinero said of Stevenson—that Hardy "had in him a large measure of dramatic talent . . . the makings of a dramatist." [20]

As one reflects on the life of Thomas Hardy, it appears inevitable that he should have been interested in drama. In a home steeped in the old traditions of Wessex, with his father's and grandfather's love of music, his mother's zest for the local ballads, and his own natural genius for dramatizing games in a neighborhood where mumming was still practiced, Hardy seems to have been destined to become an exponent of Dorset folk drama. By reading the Greek and Elizabethan dramatists, by attending the opera and theatre in London, by associating with people of the theatre, he developed his inherent interest in the stage. Like Keats he wanted to write "a few fine plays." As we have seen, his first aspiration to write poetic drama was blighted by sight of stage realities and the advice of friends, so that he was turned in another direction. But his interest in the stage lasted for almost sixty years. After writing several volumes of poetry and short stories and fifteen novels, he returned to the drama at last and lived to crown his work in verse and fiction with two extremely different poetic dramas, *The Dynasts and The Famous Tragedy of the Queen of Cornwall.*

Notes on Hardy's Interest in the Theatre

1. William Archer, *The Old Drama and the New* (New York: Dodd, Mead & Company, 1926), p. 11.
2. Aristotle, *The Poetics*, ed. S. H. Butcher (London: Macmillan and Company, 1936), p. 15.
3. Florence Emily Hardy, *The Life of Thomas Hardy* (London: Macmillan and Company, 1933), I, 27.
4. Carl J. Weber, *Hardy of Wessex* (New York: Columbia University Press, 1940), p. 8.
5. Florence Emily Hardy, *The Life of Thomas Hardy*, I, 19.
6. Ernest Brennecke, *Life of Thomas Hardy* (New York: Greenberg, 1925), p. 79.
7. Florence Emily Hardy, *The Life of Thomas Hardy*, I, 15.
8. Roger S. Loomis, *The Play of St. George* (New York: Samuel French, 1928), preface p. 9.
9. Florence Emily Hardy, *The Life of Thomas Hardy*, I, 18-19.
10. Thomas Hardy, *The Dynasts*, xi.
11. Florence Emily Hardy, *The Life of Thomas Hardy*, I, 31.
12. Hardy's letter to Mr. Robert Donald in May of 1908 concerning the memorial theatre to Shakespeare is interesting:

"I do not think that Shakespeare appertains particularly to the theatrical world nowadays, if he
ever did. His distinction as a minister to the theatre
is infinitesimal beside his distinction as a poet, man
of letters, and seer of life, but that his expression
of himself was cast in the form of words for actors
and not in the form of books to be read was an
accident of his social circumstances that he himself
despised. I would, besides, hazard the guess that he,
of all poets of high rank whose works have taken
stage direction, will some day cease altogether to be
acted, and be simply studied." Florence Emily
Hardy, *The Life of Thomas Hardy*, II, 131-2.

13. Florence Emily Hardy, *The Life of Thomas Hardy*,
    II, 207-8.

14. Sylva Norman, "Thomas Hardy" in *The Great Vic-
    torians*, edited by H. J. and Hugh Massingham
    (New York: Doubleday Doran & Co., 1932), p. 211.

15. Frank Arthur Hedgcock, *Thomas Hardy, Essai de
    Critique: Thomas Hardy, penseur et artiste* (Paris:
    Hachette & Cie, 1911), p. 1.

16. Florence Emily Hardy, *The Life of Thomas Hardy*,
    I, 57.

17. Houghton MS. By permission of the Harvard Col-
    lege Library.

18. Florence Emily Hardy, *The Life of Thomas Hardy*,
    I, 71-2.

19. Florence Emily Hardy, *The Life of Thomas Hardy*,
    II, 15-16.

20. A. W. Pinero, "Robert Louis Stevenson: The Dra-
    matist" (New York: *The Critic*, 1903).

The Dynasts

"The very vastness of the subject leaves a
possibility that one may have something to
say worth saying. . . ."

T. S. Eliot on Dante.

In the preface to the *de luxe* Mellstock edition of his
works Hardy says, "Turning now to my verse—to myself
the more individual part of my literary fruitage—I would
say, unlike some of the fiction, nothing interfered with
the writer's freedom in respect of its form or its content."
If this be true of all his poetry, his chosen medium, it
appears to be especially true of *The Dynasts,* for with
unfaltering boldness Hardy conceived and executed this
work without parallel in poetry, at least in the twentieth
century. *The Dynasts* with its width of scale chronicling
ten of the most extraordinary years in European history,
mingling narrative and dialogue, at first baffled the critics [1]
and defied classification. And Hardy's stroke of genius in
using the supernatural chorus to envelop and interpret
the sublunary events and to give universality to his panorama has scarcely ceased to surprise.

Hardy's life long preoccupation with the events of the

Napoleonic war is evident to the reader in many of his poems and especially in *The Trumpet-Major,* where Hardy found himself "in the tantalizing position of having touched the fringe of a vast international tragedy wtihout being able, through limits of plan, knowledge, and opportunity, to enter further into its events; a restriction that prevailed for many years." [2] It is perhaps not surprising but significant to note a reference to the tactics of Napoleon's campaign in Hardy's first prose fiction, the love story of the poor man and the lady. "Egbert had previously surveyed the spot and thought it suitable for the occasion, much as Wellington antecedently surveyed the field at Waterloo." [3] As early as 1891 Hardy was considering writing "A Bird's Eye View of Europe in the Nineteenth Century." He said that it may be called "A Drama of the Times of the First Napoleon." In his preface of 1903 to the first part, Hardy called *The Dynasts* merely "drama." To the edition of the complete work in 1909 he added the footnote: "It is now called Epic-drama." [4]

Hardy explains the choice of his epic material thus: "But the slight regard paid to English influence and action throughout the struggle by so many continental writers who had dealt with Napoleon's career, seemed always to leave room for a new handling of the theme which should reembody the features of this influence in their true proportion." [5] To present the role of England in its proper setting Hardy necessarily had to take all Europe for his field. Such a setting filled with the stirring events of ten years demanded a work of imagination vast in its scope and genius. "Nearly a century was to pass," Edmund Gosse says, "before there should arise a poet who, on the huge canvas of *The Dynasts,* for the first time would paint for us a panorama of the struggle not unworthy of its stupendous issues." [6]

In his zeal for historical truth, Hardy devoted years to research into the facts of the Napoleonic War. Mr. Rutland has made an interesting study to determine the extent of that research and the sources which Hardy used for *The Dynasts*.[7] Mrs. Hardy told me at Max Gate that she thought Hardy used everything available in the British Museum.[8] As a result of Hardy's zeal for accuracy and astonishing industry, the history used in *The Dynasts* remains unquestioned. So vivid are the details that the *Daily News* said that the reader would "literally see a hill hard by Waterloo fought again, and he will not find a battalion out of place or an incident out of focus."[9] Hardy's letter to Edward Clodd reveals his immersion in the subject. He wrote on New Year's Eve, 1907, "In two or three days I shall have done with the proofs of *Dynasts III*. It is well that the business should be over, for I have been living in Wellington's campaigns so much lately that, like George IV, I am almost positive that I took part in the Battle of Waterloo, and have written of it from memory."[10]

As an English historical epic *The Dynasts* is unique, and as such can probably never be superseded by a similar work on the same subject. If it were not, however, for Hardy's own sense of history, as *The Times Literary Supplement*[11] said, "the very greatness of his theme would undo him." So vivid are Trafalgar, Peninsula, and Waterloo, so brilliant the portrayal of the Duchess of Richmond's ball, and so grim the cellar scene with the deserters from Sir John Moore's Forty-Second, as Hardy writes history that Mr. Abercrombie has been led to hazard, "I should think that the average cultured person in England will henceforth take his knowledge of Napoleonic history chiefly from *The Dynasts*, just as his knowledge of

English history comes for the most part from Shakespeare's chronicles." [12]

Although Hardy wanted to pay due regard to England at war, he does not unduly flatter the English. In his admiration for Napoleon, for instance, he forgets his own country. He is unprejudiced, impersonal, detached. But as Mr. John Freeman in *London Mercury* has pointed out:

> Taking all Europe for its field, *The Dynasts* none the less is rooted in Wessex and is triumphantly English to the end. And here, at length, is the final factor in Thomas Hardy's fame; he is a purely English writer speaking to English hearts and heads. His strength and his weakness, his honesty and limitations, his humility and independence, are all alike English. He restores our decaying consciousness that our roots, too, are in the earth, and that is English earth. Intellectually he escapes the confines of the Channel, but emotionally he is completely English. [13]

Hardy was equally zealous for truth in the portrayal of his characters. The great historical personages he knew "from memories and letters and scraps of reminiscence used with the divination of the poet and the justice of the novelist." [14] In *The Dynasts* he has probably painted great men better than any other modern author. He drew them with "particularity and without parade, as if he knew them." [15] That the character of Napoleon had long appealed to him is shown by his early use of him as a character in *The Trumpet Major* and various poems. In *The Dynasts* as in *The Trumpet Major* the west country rustics talk fearfully of "Boney" and discuss breathlessly the

17

chances of invasion. And in the unpublished *Wessex Scenes from The Dynasts* which Hardy arranged for "The Hardy Players" he wrote his most vivid Napoleonic scene—one in which shepherds relate to the beacon keepers that they had seen "Boney" and an aide, actually landed in England, looking over a map by the light of a lantern. In all his works Hardy is fair to Napoleon—more fair perhaps than Tolstoi in *War and Peace*. Yet, as John Cowper Powys says, "No writer has ever dealt with the supernatural awe excited by the name of Bonaparte as mystically and intimately as he has both in *The Dynasts* and elsewhere." [16] The characterizations of Wellington, Nelson, Sir John Moore, and others are no less impressive and real. But Hardy does not limit his characters to the great personages. Rather he alternates them with Wessex rustics for whose portrayal he is unapproachable. As the *Spirit of the Years* explains, the play begins with "England's humblest hearts. Anon we'll trace its heavings in the upper coteries there." "Ay," rejoins the *Spirit Sinister,* "begin small, and lead up to the greater. It is a sound dramatic principle." By giving occasional glimpses of the untouched peasants of the West Country, Hardy portrays a more comprehensive history. They are flesh and blood and proved a good foil to the more celebrated characters. Charming as they are, the temptation, of course, would naturally be to include all of their conversation in making any abridgement of *The Dynasts* for the stage, and it is not strange that *The Nation* said of the 1920 presentation, "We all love Thomas Hardy's peasants, but in this selection they rather overbalance the tragic side." [17] That responsibility was not Hardy's. In fact, I doubt if Thomas Hardy could ever be reproached for allowing comedy to outweigh tragedy. He might have more admirers if he had! In the full text of *The Dynasts,* at any rate, the rustics are not out of proportion. They complete the picture.

Hardy did not present his characters, great and humble, as Shakespeare did, merely in their historical background. With so extensive a panorama of multitudinous events involving hundreds of characters, he realized the need of some unifying force. He achieved unity by writing the drama on three levels: the peasants and people of everyday life, the great historical figures, and the celestial chorus. The *Pities,* the *Ironies,* the *Spirit Sinister,* the *Shade of the Earth,* and the *Spirit of the Years* link up and interpret the actions and motives of those taking part in the terrestrial tragedy with the *Immanent Will.*[18] For the use of this supernatural machinery, Hardy had many forerunners in literature. His favorite *Book of Job* with the voice out of the whirlwind, *Faust* with spiritual essences used as commenting choruses, *Prometheus Unbound* both in form and content, no doubt influenced him in his handling of *The Dynasts.* And we know he had in mind the supernatural machinery of *Paradise Lost,* the *Iliad,* and *Eddas,* for he mentions them in the *Preface.* While the supernatural chorus is an artistic necessity, it proved (as we shall soon see) a practical dramatic impediment but not one so great that it could not be overcome by the genius of imagination.

The celestial abstractions have the additional value of expressing Hardy's philosophy. While he denied representing any consistent philosophy in *The Dynasts,* as in all his work, one recognizes Hardy's characteristic overtone of fatalism—deliberate or not. The spirits tell us the secret of these "flesh-hinged manikins" and how "the jacks click out their reasonings there" on earth. It is beyond my purpose to discuss *The Dynasts* as philosophy—absorbing though it is. Our interest lies particularly in the relation of such a philosophy to the drama. One can immediately see that if one presents the spectacle of the Napoleonic wars with human beings accepting and obeying the irresistible commands of the *Immanent Will,* the clash of circumstances would be lessened. If characters feel they have no freedom of will, their significance is diminished. They become merely the pawns of Fate. Indeed *if* the characters felt that they were illustrations of a deterministic philosophy the reviewer for the *London Outlook* would be correct in the following criticism:

> If you call to mind any of the great dramas in literature, *Agamemnon, Oedipus, Othello,* or *Macbeth,* you find yourself watching a conflict with destiny. Human thought and action personified in one man of heroic mould, and the inevitable consequences of human thought, and action personified for poetry as Zeus or as Fate or perhaps as other man—those are the elements of the great dramas that we know, and in the conflict . . . lies the essence of dramatic interest and suspense. The hero . . . is responsible for his own deeds, but the deed once done is irrevocable and its consequences will be what they will be. That philosophy runs through all great dramatic literature; in the choruses of *Agamemnon,* for instance, it finds expression in a thousand phrases of piteous or terrible import.

> But the philosophy on which Mr. Hardy sets out to interpret the drama of the Napoleon era seems at first sight very different. With the theory

that all human thought and action is predestined—
the expression of the *Immanent Will*—human responsibility seems to vanish, and with it, as we are
saying, the essence of dramatic interest compatible
with the attitude of mind demanded by the *Immanent Will,* the *Spirit of the Years,* and the whole
philosophic purport of the play? [19]

One is tempted to dismiss the question as *The Times*
did, "You may say, if you like, that he ought to have intended another effect, that aimed at by most plays and
achieved completely by *Oedipus Tyrannus* or *Othello;* but
to say that is merely to cut yourself off from the experience of *The Dynasts;* it does *The Dynasts* no harm." [20]
I am inclined to believe, however, that perhaps the question deserves more consideration. In the first place, we
should never forget that Hardy was dramatizing history;
and if he presents historical truth, facts known by most
of his readers, he cannot expect to achieve dramatic sus-
pense, for instance, by surprise. The reader already knows
who won the battle of Waterloo, but if he reads Hardy's
account of it, he must feel the power of the treatment
and satisfaction in the action or conflict. What the critic
for the *Outlook* seems not to realize is that the characters
do not know that the outcome is determined. Hardy
undoubtedly realized that there must be character in
drama and that "character is incompatible with the doc-
trine that human beings are simply lobules of one brain,
the *Immanent Will;*" [21] yet he seems to have considered
it sufficient for the characters themselves *to think* they are
responsible for their actions. *The Spirit of Years* says:

Deem yet man's deeds self-done, (*Fore Scene p.* 7)

With Napoleon, on the other hand, we agree that the problem is more complicated. He distinctly feels on the whole that he is ruled by the *Will* and serves the *Will*. In one place he says:

> Why hold me my own master if I be
> Ruled by the pitiless Planet of Destiny?
> Part III, Act vi, Scene iii)

And in answering Josephine he blames his star:

> Some force within me, baffling mine intent,
> Harries me onward, whether I will or no.
> My star, my star is what's to blame—not I.
> It is unswervable! (Part II, Act 1, Scene viii)

Looking on the *Spirit of the Years* observes:

> *Strange,*
> *He's of the few in Europe who discern*
> *The working of the Will.* (Part II, Act 1, scene viii)

After Waterloo, Napoleon confesses:
> Yet, 'tis true, I have ever known
> That such a Will [22] I passively obeyed!

A few lines below, on the other hand, Napoleon shows his egotistic nature and takes full responsibility for his deeds:

22

And yet—I found the crown of France in the mire,
And with the point of my prevailing sword
I picked it up! (Part III, Act vii, Scene ix)

In this respect the character is unconvincing. As Mr. Rutland says, Napoleon was either a man or a puppet of the *Immanent Will*. And it is in the lack of human responsibility and human conflict that we find the greatest artistic flaw of *The Dynasts*. If we lack conflict in the human characters, however, we find it in the abstractions. Mr. Rutland says that it is "the characterization of the Spirits which carries the whole structure." [23] They are no mere chorus. They are real personalities. They are rightfully "sources or channels of causation." [24] Although their doctrines are "tentative" and as Hardy says in the *Preface* are not warranted to "lift the burden" of this unintelligible world, they do discuss the riddle of existence and the validity of moral law.

As poetry *The Dynasts* had to win its way. Because Hardy varied his form of expression for his different types of subject matter to produce different effects one critic called the combination "nondescript." Of the 10553 lines of *The Dynasts* (excluding the stage directions and dumb shows) 1470 lines are prose, 7931 are blank verse, and 1152 are of rimed verse.[25] Hardy used prose for the peasants, the messengers, the soldiers, the servants, and occasionally for the generals. The generals, however, usually speak blank verse. Rimed verse is confined to the spirits as they sing or chant; otherwise the spirits speak blank verse or prose [26] but often close their speech with riming couplets. The songs, *The Night of Trafalgar, Budmouth Dears,* Madman's *Song* and *My Love's Gone A-Fighting* are, of course, in verse. As Edmund Gosse has pointed out, "the lyrical poetry of Mr. Hardy is not largely illustrated in *The Dynasts*, except by the choral interludes of the phantom intelligences, which have lyrical value, and by three or four lyrical songs." [27] As Hardy intended it should be, the poetry of *The Dynasts* is essentially dramatic, but it took the intelligent production of an abridgement of the play to demonstrate just how dramatic Hardy's poetry really is.

The Dynasts illustrates Hardy's capacity for visualization on a large scale. Often in the vast theatre of the Napoleonic era he projects a moving picture. Many of the stage directions and dumb shows suggest the modern cinema: "The scene is veiled," "the scene loses," "the opera house becomes lost in darkness," "the fire sinks, and snowflakes and darkness blot out all." Or "The scene changes. The exterior of the cathedral takes the place of the interior, and the point of view recedes, the whole fabric smalling into distance and becoming like a rare, delicately carved alabaster ornament. The city itself sinks into miniature . . . till clouds cover the panorama." One could add such examples indefinitely, but perhaps the most graphic is the aerial survey in the *After Scene*: "Europe has now sunk netherward to its far-off position in the *Fore Scene,* and it is beheld again as a prone and emaciated figure in which the Alps form the vertebrae, and the branching mountain-chains the ribs, the Spanish Peninsula shaping the head of the écorché. The lowlands look like a grey-green garment half-thrown off, and the sea around like a disturbed bed on which the figure lies."

Hardy's use of large crowds also suggests the cinema. He visualizes a hundred thousand infantry or twenty thousand cavalry maneuvering, or brigs and luggers at sea as many as twenty thousand sail. And in these tumultuous scenes he gives in the manner of the screen minute details where his canny eye sees dramatic action: "Further off, on the open land, bodies of troops are at field drill. Other bodies half stripped and incrusted with mud are labouring as navvies in repairing excavations. . . ."

But the chief way in which *The Dynasts* suggests a moving picture is the way it skips from place to place. In the first act of Part I, for instance, we find scenes in the following places: Wessex; Paris, the office of the Minister of Marine; London, the House of Commons; the Harbour of Boulogne; London, the House of a lady of Quality; Milan, the Cathedral. Since Hardy disregards the unity of place in this obvious manner, one credits the virtue of the suggestion that *The Dynasts* might best be presented as a moving picture.

In considering *The Dynasts* merely as drama one finds a diversity of opinion. Mr. William Lyon Phelps says:

> For *The Dynasts,* which covers the map of Europe, transcends the sky, and deals with world conquerors, is not nearly so great a world-drama as *A Pair of Blue Eyes,* that is circumscribed in a small corner of a small island, and treats exclusively of a little group of commonplace persons. Literature deals with a constant—human nature, which is the same in Wessex as in Vienna.[28]

An opposite point of view, held by the late Colonel T. E. Lawrence, was that there is nothing in English literature between Shakespeare and *The Dynasts*.[29] While not going quite so far as Colonel Lawrence, Mr. Holbrook Jackson ranked it with Shelley's *Prometheus Unbound* and Swinburne's *Atalanta of Calydon* "as one of the greatest poetic plays since Shakespeare wrote *King Lear.*" In fact, Mr. Jackson went further. "In one sense," he said, "*The Dynasts* is greater than either of its modern fellows; greater in size, in variety, and its grasp of almost every kind of character and every phase of human affairs." [30]

Although Hardy says *The Dynasts* was intended for mental performance only, it seems clear that he was, to a certain extent, thinking of the stage. He was using the artificial superstructure or machinery of the stage. There are many superficial evidences in sentences like the following: "Let the last pictures of the play be bared" and "The last act of the battle begins." There is also internal evidence in the warp and woof of his text. While *The Dynasts* is obviously not a well-made play, it is drama. It moves through the events of ten years to a great catastrophe—to a final consummation. It may be that the clash of peoples is brought about artificially, as Hardy admits in his preface and as the supernatural chorus explains, but the people do not realize that. They act in the conflict as if they were responsible human beings making their decisions on the basis of their desires and judgment.

In his criticism of the play *Tess of the d'Urbervilles* St. John Ervine said:

> The conviction I carry from his work, apart from that of his verity and bare beauty, is of intense drama. I know few works which are so essentially dramatic as *The Dynasts* despite the fact that *it can never be staged.* (italics mine) All the scenes in that immense epic move. Mr. Hardy was not attempting then to make a play which would fit the stage, but if he had made an attempt what a play he would have made! [31]

One does not question St. John Ervine's appreciation of Hardy's drama, and in one sense he is right about the staging of the play. *All* of *The Dynasts,* of course, can never be staged, but before this statement was made *parts* of it had been very effectively portrayed both in the professional and amateur theatre. And one cannot be sure that Hardy did not write it with dramatization in view. In 1914, after *The Dynasts* had been very successful at the Kingsway, *The Athenaeum* made this statement, "Mr. Hardy molded better than he knew in making the suggestion. . . . We may suppose that the vast and various extent of his own conception held him puzzled, haunted, moreover, with some memory of the staging of *Faust*." [32] The "suggestion" refers to Hardy's conclusion of his preface:

> In respect of such plays of poesy and dream a practicable compromise may conceivably result, taking the shape of monotonic delivery of speeches, with dreamy conventional gestures, something in the manner traditionally maintained by the old Christmas mummers, the curiously hypnotizing impressiveness of whose automatic style—that of persons who spoke by no will of their own—may be remembered by all who ever experienced it. Gauzes or screens to blur outlines might still further shut off the actual, as had, indeed, already been done in exceptional cases. But with this branch of the study we are not concerned here. [33]

It is my impression that Hardy was perfectly aware that he had written a work parts of which were suitable for stage production, whereas his suggestion makes it

27

clear that he realized there were parts of his drama which could not be performed realistically. If he had written his "chronicle-piece" involving merely the everyday characters and the historical personages and restricted them to stage limits, one would not have been surprised if he had sent his script to a theatrical manager. But since he restricted himself to no physical limitations less than all Europe and the enveloping sky and extended his text to nineteen acts and one hundred and thirty scenes, he obviously recognized that it would overtax the facilities of the modern stage. Therefore, rather than suggest boldly that it be presented on the stage, he offered half-apologetically this tentative suggestion of the nonrealistic manner. It was done with his characteristic self-protective instinct.

Stubbornly conservative literary taste refused for a long time to recognize *The Dynasts*. It granted Hardy preeminent place among living novelists, and was reluctant to accept him as a poet, much less a dramatist. Critics were almost agreed at the time of the appearance of *The Dynasts* that it was not on the same high level as his great novels. One even went so far as to suggest, "Now that he has completed this remarkable experiment we may hope for successors to them." [34]

Critics were mystified by the unique work. "The impression left on the mind by the first volume was one of bewilderment," [35] the critic for the *Daily News* confessed after he had seen the completed work in 1908. He said that critics had looked on the first volume as an experiment "at once so daring, so original, and so vast. . . ." [36] It was a thing from the first "to arouse a sort of astonishment and expectation." [37] Evidently when Hardy issued the first volume he indicated that the completion of the design depended upon the reception it had from the public. Shortly after the appearance of the first volume, Hardy wrote to his friend, Edward Clodd, on March 22, 1904, showing his inclination to carry the thing further:

> I did not think that *The Dynasts* would suit your scientific mind, or shall I say the scientific side of your mind, so that I am much pleased to hear that you have really got pleasure out of it. I did not mean to publish Part I by itself until quite a few days before I sent it up to the publishers, and to be engaged in a desultory way on a manuscript which may be finished in five years (the date at which I thought I might print it, complete) does not lead one to say much about it. On my return from London I had a sudden feeling that I should never carry the thing any further, so off it went. But now I am rather inclined; though I rather wish I had kept back the Parts till the whole could be launched, as I at first intended.[38]

Because his full design was not clear to the critics in Part One, Hardy was drawn into a long discussion by letter with the editor of *The Times Literary Supplement*. In his article of January 29, 1904, the editor of T.L.S. seems to have been bewildered by Hardy's "quasi-dramatic species" and suggested bad architecture in building "a book according to the methods of a play or a play according to the methods of a book." On February 5, Hardy's "Rejoiner" [39] on the subject of *The Dynasts* appeared in which he said, "I believe that any one who should sit down and consider at leisure how to present so wide a subject within reasonable compass would decide that this was, broadly speaking, *the only way*." (italics mine)

When the second volume appeared, the press showed a discernible tempering of its criticism. "The critical attitude," *Current Literature* said, "if not appreciative has at least become respectful." [40] Yet still in 1906 reviewers who had acclaimed Hardy a foremost writer of fiction were severe in their criticism of *The Dynasts* as philosophy, poetry, and drama. *The Times Literary Supplement* says:

> Mr. Hardy, indeed, is singularly devoid of the peeping graces and adornments we are accustomed to look for in a poet. Compare the blank verse of *The Dynasts* even with the musical and practical blank verse of Mr. Stephen Phillips, verse rich with a thousand associations: and it is indeed difficult at first to understand why a man of immense talent like Mr. Hardy should have chosen this particular medium of rhythm for what is perhaps his greatest book. No one was ever, apparently, more insensible to the natural magic, the delight of purely poetic language. No one has ever appeared less disposed to "look upon fine phrases like a lover." . . . To find a poetical parallel to Mr. Hardy's willful and determined plainness of language we should have to go back to Crabbe; or better still, to Wordsworth's "noble plainness." Yet here again, Mr. Hardy refuses to be classified. . . .[41]

William Archer writing in *The Tribune* (London) said:

> There can be no doubt that this is a grandiose design which Mr. Hardy is patiently, indomitably working out. Nor is it questionable that the work bears the impress of an original and powerful spirit.

. . . We may question whether *The Dynasts* will ultimately rank in English literature beside *Jude the Obscure* and *Life's Little Ironies,* and *Wessex Poems.* But, for the moment, at any rate, such questions are idle. We have to consider, not what Mr. Hardy might, could, would or should have given us, but what he has actually given us: and that is a fascinating series of dissolving views, or glimpses of history seen through the medium of a peculiar poetic temperament.[42]

After the third volume appeared critics on the whole agreed that Hardy was justified in using his allegedly dramatic form. They appreciated the magnitude of the scheme, the appeal to the imagination and the immensity of the conception. The critic of the *Daily News* said. "One needed the perspective of time and the relation of the parts in order to be able to say whether the structure was of granite or match-boarding . . . and yet as one closes the book on that wan note of hope . . . one cannot resist the conclusion that this vast panorama of history is one of the great and enduring products of our time." [43]

Even after that appreciation the critic of the *Daily News* added:

As drama, the work, with its nineteen acts and 130 scenes, is, of course, impossible for the stage. It is the drama of suggestion to which the reader brings his knowledge to fill in the gaps. . . Whether as philosophy or history or drama, *The Dynasts* must rank as a work of genius." [44]

Beyond the suggestion Hardy made in the *Preface,* we have the evidence of one of Hardy's good friends that he would have liked to see *The Dynasts* on the stage. Mrs. B. A. Crackenthorpe wrote to Lillah McCarthy, "I believe the secret of his heart is to see scenes from *The Dynasts* staged before he passes on." [45] Therefore, in 1914 when Granville Barker suggested that he might be able to produce *The Dynasts* at the Kingsway Theatre, Hardy did not hesitate to agree. His eager response to the theatre is in direct opposition to his attitude when he was asked for *Tess of the d'Urbervilles* in the 'nineties. Several reasons account for this change. When asked for *Tess* he was busy creating *The Dynasts* and did not want any outside disturbance at that time.[46] But since he had written it, he had turned to the theatre as is shown in his encouragement of the Hardy Players. For the six years preceding 1914, Hardy had been more or less active in their productions. Then four years earlier, in 1910, after he met Mr. and Mrs. Granville Barker, he had placed his confidence in their theatrical management and in Lillah McCarthy's ability as an actress to the extent that he entrusted to them his own text of *Tess of the D'Urbervilles*. Although that production did not materialize, the contact proved useful for the later production of *The Dynasts*. Mrs. Fiske's triumph in America in *Tess of the D'Urbervilles* must have made him more receptive to the idea of placing his work on the stage in England. Moreover, the timeliness of presenting a parallel European conflict in 1914 appealed to Hardy as well as to Granville Barker. But the strongest reason, of course, and the most natural one was that Hardy had written *The Dynasts* in dramatic form and he was not only willing but delighted to have it performed, especially when it was to be produced by the outstanding actor-manager of England. If anyone could do it, Granville Barker was the man.[47]

On September 25, 1914, Granville Barker wrote to Hardy from the Kingsway Theatre, Great Queen Street:

Dear Mr. Thomas Hardy,

Would you care for us to follow the run of *The Great Adventure* here with a production of *The Dynasts?* Or, rather, I fear I must say some scenes from *The Dynasts?* I do not know whether you ever considered an arrangement for the modern stage, but I have spent a little time working out the possibility as I have been able to see it, and I can extract, I find, three acts coming, roughly, from the three parts of the complete work and keeping mainly to the scenes that concern England. The first act, Trafalgar, the second, Peninsula, the third, Waterloo. If the idea does interest you, may I send for your consideration a copy so marked? [48] I hope to be able to keep some at any rate of the choruses.

Very sincerely yours,
H. Granville Barker

P.S. The Battle of Waterloo nearly stumped me, but I think I can even manage that.[49]

Hardy had appreciated for many years the work of Granville Barker.[50] And one is not surprised, therefore, by his answer:

Dear Mr. Granville Barker:

I should be much interested in your producing *The Dynasts* at your theatre. Of course, at first, I never contemplated the possibility of staging it, or any part of it, though many people have written from time to time since it came out that it might be done. And since the war broke out people write and say, "It's *The Dynasts* over again!"

I am quite willing to leave the abridgement and arrangement to you, and will examine any copy you may have marked for the purpose. I suppose that the spirits would simply be heard singing and speaking in large hollow voices from the sky. If instead of sending the scheme you are preparing you would like to come down here and stay over the night with us and talk it over, we should be delighted. Or I could run up to London for a few hours any day, should you prefer that, as I often do so.

Nothing certainly could be more apt than *The Dynasts* at the present time. And whatever the virtues or defects of its adaptation, the public and the papers would probably regard its production as so timely and patriotic that they would feel bound to make it a success. However, we will not anticipate.

Yours very sincerely,
Thomas Hardy.[51]

P.S. My wife says that if Mrs. Barker would like also to run down with you she would be much pleased—as should I.[52]

The following Monday Granville Barker wrote accepting Hardy's invitation and said that he was rejoiced at the prospect of producing something that he admired so much. At Max Gate Hardy went over Barker's proposed scheme and gave his hearty approval of it. Granville Barker must have started work immediately, for *The Dynasts* appeared at the Kingsway on November 25, 1914. Despite his denial (which is characteristic) in the following letter to Sir Sidney Colvin, November 20, 1914, Hardy collaborated to some extent in the preparation.

> We return here to find your kind invitation awaiting us. I have attended one or two rehearsals of *The Dynasts*—or rather scenes therefrom—since Granville Barker wished me to do so; but shall probably not go up again; otherwise it would have been very pleasant to call on you and Lady Colvin. The fact is, Barker is doing it entirely in his own way, and I have no responsibility. I must admit that his method is most ingenious and interesting.[53]

The selection of scenes was Barker's own, but Hardy wrote connecting links for them. He wrote on October 28, 1914: "I sent yesterday: 1. The few additional lines you asked for, to fill up time, and link scenes—with one or two other notes." [54] He also added a rousing new prologue and epilogue connecting the period of the World War I with that of 1805. As Mr. A. E. Drinkwater, Granville Barker's assistant, told a reporter before the opening of the play, "By means of the Prologue we show that as in 1805 we were not actually fighting the French nation, but only Napoleon, so we are not now fighting the Germans themselves but only against the Kaiser and the oppression of militarism." [55]

Hardy's cooperation in the production is shown in his letter of October 9, 1914, to Barker:

I am sending along the sheets up to the end of Part II.

You will of course write in the details of exits, entrances, & business generally.

At first I wrote the second part of the cellar scene as if viewed from without, with Napoleon, etc. visible, & the fugitives looking out through the window. But I altered it. I am glad you think of having him seen after all.

P.S. I have received Mr. Drinkwater's letter on business arrangements, & am answering it. It is quite satisfactory.[56]

The music of the production interested him especially. On October 28, 1914, he told Barker:

I sent yesterday: . . .

2. The music of the two songs: "Budmouth Dears" and "My Love Is Gone A-fighting."

The other song viz: "Buonaparty" (the marching song of the soldiers when the coach overtakes them), and "The Night of Trafalgar"—both in Part I, can be bought at Booseys, 295 Regent Street —so I don't send copies of them. The published titles are:

1. "Buonaparty," Song. Words by T. H., music by Ralph Vaughan Williams.
2. "Song of Trafalgar." Words by T. H., music by Cyril Scott.

If you cannot get them there, I could send a copy of them; but I suppose you will be able to do so.

I think that the more songs you have the better,

and if you like I can send the music of "Men Who March Away!", the song of the soldiers that appeared in *The Times* the other day. It might perhaps be sung between the Parts, or at the end. However you know best.

The realities of the present war are very distressing. I think you are doing the best you can in the circumstances.

Our kind regards to Mrs. Granville Barker.

Sincerely yours,
Thomas Hardy [57]

Staging *The Dynasts* naturally brought misgivings to the minds of some of the most ardent admirers of Thomas Hardy and Harley Granville Barker. Sympathetic though they were, these friends wondered how the management at the Kingsway—brilliantly intellectual though it was— could present the whole Napoleonic era in three hours in the theatre. How could Hardy's colorful panorama of battles with maneuvering armies and navies on land and sea be represented on the London stage? How could whole European courts and parliaments, as well as hundreds of *dramatis personae,* be presented to the audience? Could the earthiness of beacon keepers, the humor of infantrymen, the worldliness of generals be kept while preserving the otherworldliness of the supernatural chorus? Such questions were pertinent. These problems would seem to make Hardy's play unsuitable for any stage. To most anyone the task would seem impossible, but the word impossible was not known to Granville Barker.

Two great problems faced him. The first was that practical one of selection. Obviously a play that would require (according to a theatrical expert) a day and a night of steady playing could not be produced in its entirety—

even if it all could have been legally licensed.[58] In abridging *The Dynasts* to perhaps a tenth of its original size to bring it within the range of the theatre, Granville Barker adopted a perfectly consistent policy. He gave unity to his work by choosing only those scenes where England and the common enemy were involved. This, of course, left out all of the Russian and Austrian campaigns—Moscow, Jena, Austerlitz. It eliminated many of the most dramatic scenes, for example, those in which Josephine and Maria Louise played. This selection took away some of the significance of the title, but it was necessary to make the play playable. Mr. Barker's material included the Battle of Trafalgar, with the death of Nelson, the retreat of Sir John Moore and the 42nd to Coruña and his midnight burial, "the romance of which is so generally remembered while the unfortunate commander's skillful conduct of retreat is forgotten"; [59] the battle of Fontainebleau, Albuera and Salamanca; Napoleon's abdication; the Duchess of Richmond's Ball on the eve of Quatre-Bras, and Waterloo. And interspersed among these swelling scenes are glimpses of rural Wessex life with Hardy's West Country people.

Hardy wrote the following prologue for the play, which the Reader gave, *standing with Book in hand. . . .*

In these stern times of ours, when crimson strife
Throws shade on every thoroughfare of life,
Disfigures comely countries with its gore,
And sends back mangled heroes to our shore,
The gift of gifts is sturdy hardihood,
That holds it firm through each vicissitude,
Not only hour by hour, but year by year,
If need be, till life's lurid skies be clear.

Arrested by perceptions such as this
We gather that it may not be amiss,
During the few brief minutes you can spare,
From the unnumerable claims that call your care,

To raise up visions of historic wars
Which taxed the endurance of our ancestors;
That such reminders of the feats they did
May stouten hearts now strained by issues hid;

Therefore we have assayed to represent,
By our faint means, event upon event
That Europe saw a hundred years ago—
—What matters that Napoleon was our foe?
Fair France herself had no ambitious ends;
And we are happy in a change that tends
To make the nearest neighbors closest friends.[60]

[*Reader*] *Walks down steps and sits at his desk.*

Hardy approved of Barker's arrangement of the scenes thus:

Part I. Trafalgar
Scene I—A ridge in Wessex—March 1805
Scene II—A place near by—Summer 1805
Scene III—Another ridge in Wessex—August 1805
Scene IV—The Same—next morning
Scene V—The deck of "The Bucenature," off Tra-
        falgar—October, 1805
Scene VI—The quarter-deck of the Victory; same
        day Daybreak

39

These are the actual scenes which Granville Barker chose from the nineteen acts and one hundred thirty scenes of *The Dynasts*. These Napoleonic crises include scenes of a wide variety: scenes of comedy, tragedy, humor, and heroism. But these scenes of world tragedy, rural simplicity, and gay sophistication do not compose the whole play. These are connected by choruses given by two Muses chiefly from the *Spirit of Pities* as for instance: the "fateful phrase of the Coruña retreat," the "inspiration of Albuera," and "the pity of Nature seared and scarred by the tread of armies before Waterloo." The actual scenes are also expanded by the stage directions of Hardy's play which were given by the Reader.[61] In this way Mr. Barker could have included the motion-picture aspect of *The Dynasts*. He could even have used that description of the *Immanent Will* above the battlefield in the Russian campaign, if it had suited his purpose: "a brain-like network of currents and ejections, twitching, interpenetrating, entangling, and thrusting hither and thither the human forms." [62] By using the Muses and the Reader,[63] there was, in fact, no limit to what Mr. Barker could take from *The Dynasts*. In this way he revealed Hardy's unplayable play "as a great comprehensive entity for dramatic representation—dramatic recitative, rather, with scenes interspersed to maintain the balance of realization." [64] Certainly it is not a well-made play. The interest was in the individual scenes rather than in the whole. Mr. Allan Wade, who acted in it, wrote:

> A particular difficulty was that each scene—being so short—had to create its own atmosphere from the start—there was no chance of "working up" a scene as there is in a play of normal construction and this fact kept everybody very keen and alert throughout the run.[65]

Although it lacked climax and progression, the most severe critic of the performance admitted, "Mr. Barker has given us a spectacle, which in its content, cannot help moving us deeply." [66] Unfortunately it proved to be almost too

41

moving for war times. *The Nation* said of it even after the war—in 1920—"The whole theme was hardly endurable for its poignancy." [67] The *London World* said it did not make for the gayety of the nation. "I feel as if I had been in church," protested an old lady as she came out, "and I wondered whether it was not also a merciless production at such a time." [68] Critics agreed that Granville Barker converted Hardy's metaphysics and pessimism into something that harmonized with their own feelings at the time. "This was a difficult thing to do, and it has been done with complete success." [69] The only reason that they could bear to see such a moving drama of war in 1914 was that Hardy touched it with a wistful distance, a pity of inhuman remoteness. But even then Granville Barker had to take out the scene of the burial of Moore because of the distress it caused the spectators. [70]

Hardy expressed in his epilogue, composed for the occasion, the hope that such painful scenes of history would not be re-enacted:

> We have now set forth, in our imperfect way,
> Ten years of history, as a three hours' play,
> Leaving to your quick fancy all, or much,
> That made a stern reality of such.
>
> Yet how should art, even thus, call clearly back
> Court, camp and council, battle and bivouac,
> The din and uproar of that crushing time,
> By the mere conjurings of masque and rhyme,
> Were it not helped to-day in saddest wise
> By sudden sharp events beneath our eyes—
> Nation at war with nation, cruel wrong
> Inflicted on the weaker by the strong!

May such reminders soon forever pass,
And war be but a shade on memory's glass,
And Might uphold the injured people's cause,
And Europe move again to genial laws;
May soon succumb all influence malign,
And still the Star of England proudly shine!
                    God save the King! [71]

Granville Barker's second problem appears even more difficult than the first. "One was more impressed by the scenic impossibilities," says William Archer, "than the dramatic impossibilities of the great epic in dialogue." The problems of representing the *dramatis personae* of European courts, parliaments, and battlefields would seem difficult enough, but as Archer says in *The Nation*:

> And then there was the supernatural machinery: that hovering chorus of "Phantom Intelligences"—the Spirit of Years, the Spirit of the Pities, the Spirits Sinister and Ironic, the Recording Angels, and other fearful wild fowl,[72] to whom the poet has assigned the task of shedding upon the world-historic spectacle the searchlights of his pessimistic philosophy. How were these aerial phantasms to be treated? It might have been possible, no doubt, simply to omit them; but to this Mr. Hardy would hardly have consented; and besides, the action without its lyric accompaniments would have been like a libretto without music.[73]

This, no doubt, was the problem that taxed Granville Barker's energy and scenic skill as a manager. To unfold in a limited theatre a drama which Hardy conceived in a theatre having none of the physical restrictions of ordinary stagecraft demanded a new type of dramatic art. Granville Barker had no precedent for staging *The Dynasts,* but as he was never afraid of experiment, he mastered the difficulties involved by devising a new technique. He solved the problem with admirable tact and ingenuity.

The performance of *The Dynasts,* visible and invisible, was rightly conceived throughout. Realism and realistic scenery were out of the question, for as Pellinore in *The Referee* says:

> Steam, coloured lights, the rapid explosion of guns, the mimic representations of battles, perhaps even a tableau of a British square at Waterloo repulsing Ney's cavalry charges, would have been belittling to the magic of the poetry and even ludicrous. There is no attempt to create a spectacular appeal or to foster the spirit of pageantry. . . .[74]

The stage itself was divided by plinth-like pillars. There was an especially constructed proscenium of plain grey, filled in with grey curtains. Against each of the panels of the proscenium was placed an elevated throne; while from the narrow apron in front of the curtains converging flights of steps led down to a stone seat with a sort of stone lectern before it, at which the Reader sat, while on each side of the proscenium were seats occupied by the two actresses who, as Strophe and Antistrophe, acted as a sort of Greek chorus. Otherwise there was no decoration except what the costumes and uniforms of the Napoleonic era offered. Between the pillars there was a recessed and curtained embrasure where, on a slightly raised inner stage, the intimate scenes were acted.

Archer described the opening of the play thus:

"And the action of the drama is explained to the audience by a Reader who is established at a desk immediately below the stage. The Reader, indeed, suggests a lecturer, or a *confrerencier;* to him is left the task of expatiating upon the terrific operations in which Nelson, Wellington, and Napoleon are engaged." [75] The Reader delivers the thrilling message of Nelson, "England expects. . . ." It is the Reader who announces the fall of Scott, the wounding of Nelson, the victory at Cape Trafalgar, Pitt's speech at the Guildhall, Wellington's next move, Ney's attack, the death of Picton, the abdication of Napoleon and the victory at Waterloo. "It is the grey-robed chorus who discourse and moralize upon the defeat and downfall of Napoleon." [76]

The striking simplicity of the production with subdued lights was appropriate, and the architectural proportions were pleasing; but the *London World* had these comments:

The claim made upon the imagination produced something like nervous exhaustion for some. We were bewitched into seeing a whole battlefield in a perfectly blank gray curtain, from which came voices. One felt the cold night air, and the sound of the distant sea came faintly to one's ears when they laid Sir John Moore's body in his lonely grave, although there was no scenery but a little heap of earth and a dank black cloth. A brilliant piece of work, reflecting the greatest credit upon all concerned, and setting a seal upon the originality and daring of Miss Lillah McCarthy and Mr. Granville Barker—for no one else would have attempted it. . . .[77]

The Reader also links the scenes and conducts the audience from place to place. He says, "We next find ourselves at King George's watering place again; and we enter the 'Old Rooms' inn." Or at the end of the first act:

Meanwhile the month moves on to counter-deeds,
   Vast as the vainest needs,
And fiercely the predestined plot proceeds.

In the manner of the Chorus in *Henry Fifth,* the Reader transports the audience across the channel in Act III: "To follow our plan of personally conducting you through space and time to each cardinal scene of this eventful drama, we must cross the Channel again to Brussels, and enter the famous ball-room there on the night of the fifteenth of June ensuing. It is nearly twelve o'clock. The Duke and Duchess of Richmond are the Host and Hostess."

Presently the curtains opened in the middle and through them came two stately muse-like ladies (Miss Esmé Beringer and Miss Carrie Haase), who proceeded to occupy the two thrones, and Mr. Henry Ainley,[78] in Georgian attire, with a gray academic gown, who stepped down and seated himself at the lectern, facing the audience. To these three personages, the dual chorus and the single Reader, were assigned the lyrical, philosophical, and narrative portions of the production. The two Muses, as they naturally would, spoke in verse, while the Reader, speaking for the most part in prose, supplied what may be called the connective tissue for the episodes, or the thread on which they were strung. He read, in short, Mr. Hardy's elaborate and characteristic stage-directions.[79]

In this scenic framework, the drama of Napoleon, Wellington, and Nelson was enacted. This organ for epic-dramatic expression, alternating narration with dialogue, allowed for many of the incidents off stage in the imagination of the audience. One critic said, "It says much for Mr. Ainley's magnificent reading, and for the cleverness of the actors on the stage, that after the first strangeness of the experience had passed off, the illusion created itself quite naturally in the minds of the audience." [80] In this way, with no attempt at realism, the battles of Trafalgar, the Peninsula, and Waterloo are fought and won without the smoke and fire and din of battle.[81] Granville Barker's manner of production of *The Dynasts* attests the truth of Sir Cedric Hardwicke's statement, "so long as the imagination is set alight by fine acting and fine writing, the action of a play can encompass anything." [82]

In this manner Granville Barker accomplished what was hitherto considered impossible. His production was generally considered (*The Spectator* notwithstanding) a feat of imagination and artistry which in no way lessened the grandeur of Hardy's poetic drama. On the other hand, it heightened it, or at least many critics appreciated, if not for the first time, at least more than ever before, Hardy's genius not only as a poet but as a dramatist. One critic wrote:

But those of Mr. Hardy's admirers who had the good fortune to be present at the Kingsway Theatre the other day when Mr. Granville Barker placed *The Dynasts* on the stage will have found still more emphatic evidence of Mr. Hardy's genius as a poet. It was not a great first night as such things are managed by Sir Herbert Tree and Sir George Alexander, functions where everybody who is anybody is present. Among the audience, it is true, I caught sight of Mr. H. G. Wells and Mr. Masefield, but I have seen more of our men of letters on occasion at a musical comedy than I saw at Mr. Granville Barker's great production. The three volumes of *The Dynasts* is a record of events in European history that have thrilled the select band of literary enthusiasts who love great drama. *The Dynasts* placed Mr. Hardy in the front rank of our poets as *The Return of the Native* placed him in the front rank of our novelists.

Had anyone told me, however, that here in *The Dynasts* was an acting play I should have been utterly incredulous, and my admiration for Mr. Granville Barker is enhanced tenfold in that he was able to take these three volumes and carve them down into a fine acting play. He was able to bring together a company which declaimed this verse in such a manner as to carry the conviction that one was listening to a great dramatic performance, a performance, moreover, vastly superior to any of the poetic dramas to which we have been treated during the past ten years or so.[83]

What the presentation at the Kingsway did more than anything else was to bring out the dramatic quality of the action. The scenes were staged and played to perfection. "The impression remains," according to *The Athenaeum,* "that this play may well stir the imagination and

48

steel the heart more than any other representation of English language and greatness; and never more so than now." [84] It proved that dramatic success does not consist of clever curtains and trifling bits of ingenuity, but rather upon an interesting theme, with characters in action and interesting dialogue illustrating and developing it. Reviewers saw that Hardy had the dramatic essentials and that Granville Barker brought them successfully to the stage.

> Mr. Barker has shown that *The Dynasts* does and must exist for its greater strength, *as a visible and audible elevation* (italics mine). Secondly, he has comprehended the proportions to be observed in a version limited by theatrical conditions. In fact, he has done for Mr. Hardy very much what Boito did for Goethe: he has seen the work as a complete whole, and then as a reduced whole. [85]

The leading article in the Christmas number of *The Times Literary Supplement*, December 18, 1914, sums up the whole situation:

> *The Dynasts* on the stage is thoroughly dramatic, and it proves that a closet-drama cannot be even good closet-drama unless it will act well. The imagination which makes good reading in dialogue also makes good acting, for the dialogue cannot be well imagined without the action that causes it and results from it. Mr. Hardy has imagined both; and as his scenes are interesting to read, so they are interesting when acted.

The critic further points out that a play does not need

to be well made to be good and that *The Dynasts* gives coherence by assuming a knowledge of the history of the time. It agrees that this form of art would not suit an "invented story" but works well with such characters as Nelson and the Duke of Brunswick.

Still, a bad writer would only expose his inadequacy to so great a theme, and we should resent his attempt to take advantage of it. But it may be said of Mr. Hardy that he has made his characters out of great men more successfully than any writer known to us, and he has succeeded just because he has not tried to get a literary advantage of them.

Assuming the greatness of Napoleon, Nelson, and Wellington,[86] Hardy proceeded with the business in hand without talking about their greatness. What they did and said interested the audience even if said in the rhetorical manner of an Elizabethan chorale.

We read, in fact, to see what they will say or do, and the poetry is only a means of conveying that to us and of conveying their thoughts better than ordinary speech could convey it. There is, as in all good poetic drama, a constant effort to reveal the whole man to us and not merely so much as might be revealed by action and speech to an ordinary observer in real life. But whatever is revealed is dramatic and tells upon the stage no less than when it is read . . . but *The Dynasts* on the stage proves, if it needed proving, what life, what justice, what essential rightness there is in his conception of characters and situations. For if there were not, the play, lacking as it does all theatrical contrivance, would be dead; whereas it seems to give life to the actors rather than be brought to life by them. It has always been the quality of a good play that it forces us to forget the actor in the part, even when he is too much of an actor. The compelling power of the whole is so strong that, even in those short scenes chosen out of it, we feel the sequence of the vast dark background of history, as if in every scene a searchlight were thrown for a moment, now upon one, now upon another spot in the stream of events. And this sense of sequence and vastness could not be given to us if Mr. Hardy had not the power, shared by Shakespeare and Tolstoy of making his characters live and his events move the moment his scene begins. He always keeps to business, because he knows what his business is, because he has both knowledge and a clear design; and if he lacked these no beauty of words and no poetic ornament could make his drama live.[87]

The general conclusion of the critic of *The Times Literary Supplement* is that *The Dynasts* triumphed over a lack of theatrical contrivance by being a representation of momentous action and that it "acts even better than it reads." [87]

The Dynasts, then, is a great achievement; and the performance of it proves it greater even than we thought. So we are grateful to Mr. Granville Barker for it; and not merely for what he has done, but also for the promise of what may be done in the future. For *The Dynasts,* though not written for the stage, may tell our poetic dramatists how they ought to write for the stage; how the essence of large poetic drama is not poetry of curtains, but revealing action and words to suit it. Mr. Hardy writes blank verse, which is supposed to be outworn, and often it is rhetorical blank verse which ought to be the most obsolete of all; but, because he says it in what reveals the minds of the speakers, it is as much alive as the dialogue of Ibsen. Therefore the business of the poetic dramatist is not to trouble too much about the kind of speech or verse that he will use—he must use the best he can find for his purpose—but to know his characters and their actions. Still less need he trouble to be theatrical or to produce a little-minded play. He is not likely to combine vividness and cumulative power as they are combined in *King Lear*. But he must remember that drama is action, and that poetic drama is momentous action; and he must see his drama as action and fit his speech to that. That is what Mr. Hardy has done, and that is why his drama acts even better than it reads.[89]

This production, then, as we have seen, is important to the theatre, to Hardy, and to literature. It also has the distinction of marking the end of Granville Barker's career as an actor-manager in England. St. John Ervine says, "Granville Barker's brave venture at the Kingsway and the Savoy came to an abrupt end, but not before he had endeavored to keep the theatre out of the midden by producing scenes from *The Dynasts*. Like Job, Granville Barker could say 'Changes and war are against me.'" [90]

Oxford Production

"Not the least valuable and delightful of Oxford's many 'impossible loyalties' is the austere persistency with which, despite the rest of the nation, she regards the drama as an influence of education," wrote Max Beerbohm in 1900 after seeing *Twelfth Night* at Oxford. "There," he said, "all the histrionic genius and latent talent of the undergraduates is jealously preserved by the Vice Chancellor for the annual bout of classic drama." [91] This tradition of classic drama was maintained by the Oxford University Dramatic Society from its founding in 1884 until the outbreak of the first World War. In the spring of 1914 the Oxford University Dramatic Society presented *The Acharnians* and then for almost five years ceased to be. But after the long interruption of war, when something like normal life returned to the universities, the O.U.D.S. feebly renewed its activity. Charles Morgan, who was manager of the 1920 production, described the condition of the Society in 1919:

> The tradition was broken, the surviving membership was not more than half a dozen, and the treasury was empty. During 1919 new members joined and new life began to flicker in the Society, but its future largely depended upon the success or failure of the first annual play in the new series.
>
> An undergraduate was instructed to consider, during the long vacation of 1919, what play should be performed and report to the Committee. His

choice was *The Dynasts*. And he had to defend it against those who objected that it was not Shakespearian and that Shakespeare was a tradition of the Society: and against those more dangerous critics who said that *The Dynasts* would be costly, and pointing to the balance-sheet, asked whence the money would come. The financial objection was at last overcome by personal guarantees.[92]

The battle between *The Dynasts* and Shakespeare was waged through the long vacation. On the first of September at the Royal Automobile Club the undergraduates of the Oxford University Dramatic Society agreed that the choice should rest between *Macbeth, Othello, Hamlet,* and *The Dynasts.* Later that evening in the Alhambra, Charles Morgan said to Maurice Colburne, "If we don't do *The Dynasts,* I shall be so disappointed that I shan't be able to get up any interest for what we do do." [93] The battle finally narrowed to *The Dynasts* and *Hamlet.* The cause for *Hamlet* was sustained by C. K. Allen; that of *The Dynasts,* by Charles Morgan. C. K. Allen's argument in favor of Shakespeare was: "*Hamlet* is an essentially intellectual part. Oxford ought to be able to produce the right type of mind for *Hamlet* (which the ordinary actor-manager certainly has not). . . . It would be interesting to see Hamlet played by a really young man, as there is every reason to suppose that Hamlet himself was young. In fact, he had only just used to be an undergraduate. . . ." [94] Charles Morgan's argument pointed out the appropriateness of *The Dynasts:*

"*The Dynasts* may not be produced again in our lifetime. Shakespeare being dead and being a textbook classic, all the comfortable people are ready

54

to do lip service to him; but Hardy is alive, is the greatest of living men, is the only living Englishman who we know with absolute certainty is immortal; and we think we might gracefully pay some tribute to him. He is a very old man and unless we do it speedily we may be too late. . . ." [95]

The committee of serious undergraduates— most of whom had taken part in the war—recognized the absolute fitness of Hardy's great historical drama and, despite the traditions of the university and the financial obstacle, endorsed the choice of the undergraduate, evidently Charles Morgan himself. The vice chancellor, Dr. Blakiston of Trinity, too, could not shut his eyes to the claims of *The Dynasts*. He, therefore, gave a special permission for the play even though it was not on the list open to the Society, inasmuch as it was by a living writer. And fortunately it developed later that some of the old members of the famous Society supported the tremendous undertaking.

Mr. Arthur Bourchier, Mr. Holman Clark, and others—with the help of some eminent actors and actresses—rallied to the cause, and gave recently in the New Theatre, Oxford, a gala performance which set the Society on its legs again. Already the great plan for the spring production had been formed. . . . [96]

Months before the plans developed thus far the committee faced what is considered its most serious difficulty. "The play was copyright, and it seemed to us very probable that Hardy would refuse permission to perform it," Charles Morgan wrote later. "He is an old man, we said,

55

and set fast in Dorset; he will not give a fig for what he will call amateur theatricals, nor will he be troubled about our affairs. It was the impression of all of us that he would be forbidding and formidable, and he was approached with misgiving." [97]

Maurice Colbourne, the president of the Oxford University Dramatic Society, wrote to Hardy during the Michaelmas term on October 20, 1919:

> Dear Mr. Hardy,
> I am wondering whether you will be interested to hear that *The Dynasts* has been having a drawn out battle with *Hamlet* and *Macbeth* throughout the Long Vac," [98] and last Sunday won easily. For on that date the O.U.D.S. committee decided, subject to your blessing, to produce *The Dynasts* during the O.U.D.S. week. . . .[99]

To one who has followed Hardy's attitude toward the theatre, professional and amateur, since his writing *The Dynasts,* it would have seemed uncharacteristic and indeed surprising if Hardy had refused the Oxford Committee "the big blessing and good wishes" which Maurice Colbourne said they awaited. Hardy never despised the amateur. In fact, he seems to have preferred the amateur to most professional performances with their conventions and artificialities. And Hardy always preferred a great theme handled even inadequately to a slight one with the best of technique. One can understand why he would not only be pleased to have *The Dynasts* revived after the war but why he would be flattered to have these undergraduates who had just participated in a similar tragedy challenge their traditions to produce his play. The realization of their experience may have been the cause of his saying

56

that he wondered at their having chosen it. At any rate, Charles Morgan says:

> He gave us the play, not grudgingly nor with an air of patronage, but with so gracious a courtesy that we were made to feel that he was genuinely pleased to find young men eager to perform his work. I do not remember the text of his reply to the original request, but I remember well the impression made by it—an impression increased by his later correspondence. Long before he came to Oxford his individuality had become established among us. Without whittling away his legend by any of the affectations of modesty, he had, by his gentle plainness, banished our fear of it.[100]

Hardy wrote Colbourne on October 20, 1919:

> I knew nothing about the suggestion that *The Dynasts,* or rather, scenes from *The Dynasts* (for you cannot act it all) should be produced by the O.U.D.S. but I have great pleasure in agreeing to your trying your hand on it if you and your friends care to honour the work by doing so.
>
> Mr. Granville Barker's selections were very cleverly and judiciously made, and I think you are wise in not attempting another version. . . .[101]

Before writing to Hardy, Maurice Colbourne had consulted Granville Barker. The Committee desired to use his acting version as none of them had time to arrange one. And since Granville Barker would be out of the country at the time of production, they had asked Mr. A. E. Drinkwater, an old Merton College man, who had directed the original presentation at the Kingsway, to direct the play. All this Maurice Colbourne related to

Hardy and asked him for suggestions and improvements. On November 11, 1919, Hardy wrote to Colbourne:

Your plan for showing the out-of-door scenes is very ingenious and attractive—and more elaborate than I imagined, my idea having been just a backcloth coloured greyish-blue, and a floorcloth coloured greenish-grey—a purely conventional representation for all open-air scenes. . . .

My feeling was the same as yours about Strophe and Antistrophe—that they should be unseen, and as if speaking from the sky. But it is as you hint, doubtful if the two ladies will like to have their charms hidden. Would boys do instead, or ugly ladies with good voices?

Mr. Drinkwater also wrote to me about the Prologue and Epilogue; and I have suggested to omit either all the former, or all except the lines beginning "We'll close up time as a bird its Van" [102] which are in the original book; and the Epilogue having been so entirely temporary (pertaining to the war) should I think be quite left out. Should you really need an Epilogue the Choruses beginning "Last as first the question rings" [103] might do.

But I do not wish to influence largely your methods of presentation. It will be of the greatest interest to me, whether I can get to Oxford or not, to see how the questions that arise in doing the thing have been grappled with by younger brains than mine.

Believe me,
Yours sincerely,
Thomas Hardy [104]

According to the following letter to Hardy from Mrs. B. A. Crackenthorpe, December 5, 1919, we see that she had a hand in the selection of *The Dynasts:*

The man who is "producing" [105] it is a very remarkable young fellow—Charles Morgan—who is now an undergraduate at Brasenose Coll.—He was first of all in the Navy, but, at his own desire came out, and is now up at Oxford preparing for the law—I begged him last summer to, at once, read *The Dynasts*—which for me has always been one of *the* books written in my time. He was as "fired" by it as I intended he should be, and the result is that it is to be given by the "Oxford University Dramatic Society" in February next— The Committee are *wild to get you and Mrs. Hardy to come and see it.*

The Committee are confident that the Prince of Wales will most certainly come, however many engagements he may have, if only he is assured that *Thomas Hardy* will be there.

Forgive me—I do hope you are well? My warm regards to your wife—
Yours very sincerely,
B. A. Crackenthorpe [106]

Hardy yielded to the many requests to go to Oxford for the performance. In a letter of December 11, 1919, he accepted the offer of Charles Morgan to send a car to fetch Mrs. Hardy and him, although he said that it was unnecessary, and stating that they would return independently. (Later, however, he decided to go by train.) He refused to make a speech at Oxford or "even the tenth part of one." But he expressed his pleasure in the fact that *The Dynasts* was materializing at the university. He wrote:

As to the details of representation. Rather than impose any conditions of method, what I should prefer would be that your committee exercise your own judgment thereon; it would greatly interest me to see what younger and more vigorous minds than my own had decided to do in the various problems that arise. So please consider yourselves quite free-handed in any questions that occur. Certainly give more of the choral passages if you think the audience will stand them without being bored. Those selected at the Kingsway were not selected by me. I like, too, the idea of concealing the Reader as well as Strophe and Antistrophe. But it will be advisable to try the effect of all this before deciding.

There is, by the way, one more point I may mention. Mr. Barker after a few representations omitted two (I think) scenes, of his stage selection, because of the distress they seemed to cause those among the spectators who had lost relatives in the war. The scenes were two of the best—the Burial of Moore, and another, I am not sure which. . . . This I should advise you not to do.

Yours very truly,
Thomas Hardy [107]

Charles Morgan replied to Hardy's suggestions as follows:

Woodhurst
Kenley
Surrey
Sunday, December 14, 1919.

Dear Mr. Hardy,

I am very grateful for your letter, which I will show to the President of the O.U.D.S. The play is being produced for us by Mr. A. E. Drinkwater, who is Mr. Barker's manager at the Kingsway; and I will tell him of your advice about the Burial of Moore. We had decided to omit this scene, but I hope it is not too late to revise the acting version.

When I have seen the President and Mr. Drinkwater, I will write again and tell you what arrangements are being made. Your wishes, as regards a speech, will, of course, be strictly observed. I expect it will be impossible to prevent the audience from "calling" for you when you are in the theatre, but we will make it clear that there is to be no speech.

There may be difficulty with regard to the invisibility of Strophe and Antistrophe. Because these parts are of so great importance we are not entrusting them to amateur ladies, and they are to be played by Laura Cowie and probably Esmé Beringer.[108] As they are giving their services, we dare not be too dictatorial, and they may object to being invisible. Moreover, the Oxford stage is old-fashioned, and it may prove impossible to hide the speaker without spoiling the carrying power of the voice. With many thanks for your consideration of us, I am,

Yours very truly,
Charles Morgan [109]

With the exception of the Prologue and the Epilogue, the acting version of *The Dynasts* used at Oxford seems to have been the same as Granville Barker's. Despite Hardy's request for the scene showing the midnight burial of Sir John Moore, the Oxford program omits it. It may have been that the suggestion made on December 11, 1919, came too late for the committee to alter its plan, as Charles Morgan indicated to Hardy. It may have been considered, as in London, that the emotion was too poignant—too distressing for the audience. The undergraduates no doubt realized that, for a large part of the audience who, like themselves, had just participated in a real drama of greater magnitude than that represented by *The Dynasts,* the presentation would carry a degree of conviction not exclusively artistic. And consequently they excluded the burial of Moore. I gathered a more important reason from Maurice Colbourne, who said that since they already had one death scene, namely Nelson's, they did not want to use another. Hence they chose the scene of the more important character.[110]

Oxford not only borrowed Granville Barker's technique but, as we have seen, employed his manager at the Kingsway, Mr. A. E. Drinkwater, as director. Ripe in his knowledge of the original production of *The Dynasts,* it was natural for Mr. Drinkwater to follow Granville Barker's lead. In the correspondence between Hardy and Maurice Colbourne we have seen that they preferred to have the Strophe and Antistrophe concealed, so that the voices would seem to come from the sky. Hardy suggested the same for the Reader. For the reasons Charles Morgan indicated, Oxford did not adopt this suggestion. At any rate, the effect gained by showing the Reader, Strophe, an Antistrophe was impressive. "Mr. R. L. A. Harris of New College was a winning figure in a black cassock, who imparted just the right air of composure into his fine recital of the vivid words in which the action of the play is described, and which sketch the scenery of the play in a manner which almost obviates the necessity of 'staging'." [111] And of Miss Laura Cowie and Miss Joan Buckmaster (later Viscountess), who were the Spirits of Poetry, *The Observer* says:

> In their long straight robes and veiled heads they looked very mysterious, very beautiful (and sometimes very like each other). And what noble stuff they had to speak: How intensely Hardyish, for instance, that passage on the birds and insects and the animals on the eve of Waterloo! They spoke this and all else worthily, giving the sense of harmony, not of competition.[112]

And *The Times Literary Supplement* which is usually very critical of the way poetry is read—calling it a lost art—admitted that the ladies who read the spirit of poetry at Oxford "were much better at it than most professional actresses; they observed rhythms and did not overemphasize every other word. . . ." [113]

In the matter of scenery, it appears that Oxford may have improved on the London production, especially in removing columns and architraves from out-of-door scenes. Hardy himself had not approved of them in the Waterloo scene. *The Times Literary Supplement says:*

For one thing, the difficulties of scenery are happily so great that no attempt can be made to overcome them. The scenery at Oxford, if it seldom had beauty, was right in principle, just enough to show what kind of place was intended and no more. So the drama could pass from scene to scene quickly, almost as quickly as the narrative of *War and Peace;* and speed is the essence of performance in this as in all chronicle plays.[114]

While one can hardly go so far as *The Observer* and say that *The Dynasts* is "almost entirely Oxford's own work," one should point out that the members of the cast were nearly all connected with Oxford. A few days before the performance *The Observer* said:

> The cast will include Miss Laura Cowie and Miss Dorothy Warren (who is to play the same part she played at the Kingsway; but Miss Warren is herself "Oxford," being a niece of Sir Herbert Warren, the President of Magdalen. Sir Herbert, if we remember aright, succeeded Mr. J. W. Mackail as Professor of Poetry; and Mr. Mackail's son, Mr. Denis Mackail, is designing the scenery. Mr. M. D. Colbourne, the President of the O.U.D.S., will play Nelson, and another undergraduate, Mr. H. R. Barton, will play Napoleon.[115]

The Dynasts proved to be not only possible for amateurs but easier than a play "of skillfully contrived situations." *The Times,* however, commented rather severely on the acting:

It was not taken quite so fast as it might have been because some of the principal actors had unfortunately learned professional tricks; they tried to act, between their lines, instead of saying them and acting to them; they were restless in gesture and expression, not trusting to their words and the event to produce the needed effect. They had not resolved to give an amateur performance with its own peculiar merits, and so were most amateurish where they tried to be most professional. Mr. G. W. Sich, as Wellington, but for a little fidgeting, was an exception. He saw that Mr. Hardy meant his Wellington to be a contrast to Napoleon, an English, or as Mr. Shaw would say, an Irish contrast to continental over-consciousness and contrivance; so he behaved at Salamanca like a master of foxhounds; it was startling and a little ridiculous but very near to Hardy and Creevey's Wellington, and perhaps to Wellington himself. Some of the rustics, too, were too rustic according to stage conventions, they drew out their parts with pottering and doddering. If all the words had been allowed to speak themselves, more of the drama might have been acted; but we say this only in hopes of another performance of *The Dynasts* and many performances of other great plays, all by amateurs behaving like amateurs, and perhaps in time establishing a new and right way of acting that might even have its effect upon the theatre.

Where this performance excelled was in crowd scenes, like the Guildhall scene after Trafalgar, and still more the dreadful scene of deserters from the retreat to Coruña. That was magnificently done, with all the players not drilled into their parts but drawn into them, inspiring each other to a climax. We have never seen anything so well done by professionals, though the same scene was good enough in London.[116]

It seemed incredible to the critic of *The Observer* that the play could have been put together to run so smoothly with no more than three weeks of rehearsal. Surely, he said, "Mr. Drinkwater . . . must have worked wonders; but even Mr. Drinkwater could not have worked those wonders without cooperation—not only energetic but intelligent—from every member of the great company." And he admitted that he could not do justice to the actors in Hardy's great play at Oxford "unless we can find room for a hundred names or more." [117] "Three players stood out from the rest"—for the reporter of the *Christian Science Monitor*—"the Wellington of Mr. G. W. Sich (Magdalen College), the Sir John Moore of Mr. C. E. Morgan (Brasenose College), and the excellently comic 'gentleman next door' of Mr. R. L. Bradley (Oriel)." [118]

All the critics were impressed, as they could not fail to be, by the absolute appropriateness of *The Dynasts*. The drama "told most" according to *The Times Literary Supplement* "because of the time of its performance and the character of the performers and a great part of their audience." [119] The success of the eight performances at Oxford proved the wise choice of the play with which to celebrate the revival of the Oxford University Dramatic Society. The *Current History* says:

> The Oxford performance of the Hardy drama achieved what so few professional performances of great plays accomplish. Like other great works of

art, it made the audience think greatly—"not of ourselves . . . but of mankind." "That," The *Times* critic says, "is the unspoken lesson of *The Dynasts;* and in it we see the power of the English people. It was received as it was meant, not as flattery to England past or present, but as a statement of the truth about England at War." It proved more impressive than the conventional hackneyed themes of the current drama, and it is better to attempt the seemingly impossible than to surrender to the conventionally petty.[120]

The Times Literary Supplement emphasizes the universal truth of the play:

> Again and again there were strokes applauded for their likeness to reality, things said on the battlefield, in the crowd, which were recognized to be true, and by those who knew their truth only too well. The mind of the fighting man, and the mind of a people at war, are given with the justice and truth of a poet, not patriotically but universally. It is England itself because the author has not been a propagandist but an artist, seeking the universal truth in the particular and finding it.[121]

The Dynasts marked a new epoch in the history of dramatics at Oxford. With it the O.U.D.S. was firmly reestablished. And again critics were reminded of the dramatic quality of Hardy's massive drama. *The Nation* aptly asked, "What other modern treatment of war has been so little dimmed by the immensity of the conflict through which the world has just passed?" [122] And one is led to wonder when the world will produce another genius with imagination and philosophy enough to portray the first or, indeed, the second World War so dramatically.

Comparison of the Kingsway and Oxford productions would be futile as well as unfair. We should naturally expect that Granville Barker could do the play more artistic justice than was possible at the university, but as the *Christian Science Monitor* has pointed out, "To say that these undergraduates did nothing to belittle the grandeur of Hardy's conception, if they did not at all times express it, is to pay them a real compliment." [123] There is no question that they gave a creditable performance. It was an "interesting even an absorbing entertainment." [124] Hardy himself must have enjoyed it, for he was seen applauding the impersonators of Napoleon, Nelson, and Wellington. "Altogether it was an inspiring occasion," said the *Christian Science Monitor*. "One thought of the many English actors like Arthur Bouchier and H. B. Irving, who first won their laurels in playing for the same society, and in the same theatre. And one was thrillingly conscious all the time of the little man sitting rather inconspicuously in the third row of the stalls, Mr. Thomas Hardy." [125]

Hardy showed his appreciation to Maurice Colbourne in his letter of February 20, 1920:

It is a pleasure to hear from you about the wind-up of the play week—such a delightful break in a long winter.

I knew, of course, that the small hitches unavoidable on a first night would vanish later, though for that matter, I did not mind them looking on as a naive spectator to enjoy what the O.U.D.S. had provided. It is seldom that a practical company of players can hold a house in such breathless stillness as your performance did frequently. . . ." [126]

The last time *The Dynasts* was seen on the stage was at Oxford,[127] but its success in the theatre was not forgotten. Five years later Mr. J. C. Squire suggested, "Mr. Ridgeway might do worse, after *Tess*, than to give us a revival of *The Dynasts*, which was played at the Kingsway early in the war. It was an episodic chronicle, full of historical scenes (such as the Death of Nelson) as vivid as anything ever seen on the stage." [128]

Notes on The Dynasts

1. Cf. William R. Rutland, *Thomas Hardy* (Oxford: Basil Blackwood, 1938), p. 277.
2. *Preface* to *The Dynasts*, vii.
3. *An Indiscretion in the Life of an Heiress* (London, privately printed, 1934), p. 23. The Houghton Library description of this book is as follows: *An Indiscretion in the Life of an Heiress* is an adaptation by the author of his first novel, *The Poor Man and the Lady,* which was never published. The manuscript of the latter was destroyed before his death, and no copy remains. This version appeared in the *New Quarterly Magazine* for July, 1878, but was not published in book form. The present edition consists of 100 copies of which this is No. 4. Signed F.E.H.
   In the interview of George Meredith with Thomas Hardy, Meredith advised Hardy not to publish the manuscript. Years later Hardy said the only exact words he remembered of Meredith's were: "Don't nail your colours to the mast just yet." *G.M.: A Reminiscence* by T. Hardy, published at the University Press, Cambridge, Nov. 21, 1927.
4. *Preface* to *The Dynasts*, p. xi, Wessex ed.

5. *Preface* to *The Dynasts,* p. viii, Wessex ed.
6. *Public Opinion,* February 5, 1915, p. 143—quoted from *Edinburgh Review.*
7. Cf. William R. Rutland, *Thomas Hardy,* Chapter VII, "The Poems and *The Dynasts*" for sources.
8. "Once," Mrs. Hardy remarked, "he told me that he was going to give me a list of the material he used, but he never did." The original MS. in the British Museum has a footnote saying: "It is intended to give a list of the chief authorities at the end of the Third Part." The footnote is to the sentence ending "my indebtedness for detail to the abundant pages of the historian, the biographer, and the journalist, English and foreign, has been, of course, continuous." p. viii, Wessex ed. The list, however, is not there.
9. *Daily News,* February 17, 1908.
10. Thomas Hardy, *Notes on The Dynasts* (Edinburgh, printed for private circulation only, 1929). Houghton Library.
11. *The Times Literary Supplement,* February 19, 1920.
12. Lascelles Abercrombie, *Thomas Hardy,* pp. 219-20.
13. John Freeman, "Thomas Hardy," *The London Mercury,* March, 1928, p. 543.
14. *The Times Literary Supplement,* February 19, 1920.
15. *Ibid.*
16. *Current History,* March 27, 1928; p. 831.
17. *The Nation,* February 14, 1920.
18. Hardy's letter to Clodd, *Notes on "The Dynasts"* by Thomas Hardy (Edinburgh, printed for private circulation only, Houghton Library), gives pertinent comment on the Will: "What you say about the 'Will' is true enough, if you take the word in its ordinary sense. But in the lack of another word to

express precisely what is meant a secondary sense has gradually arisen, that of effort exercised in a reflex of unconscious manner. Another word would have been better if one could have it, though 'Power' would not do, as power can be suspended or withheld, and the forces of nature cannot. However, there are inconsistencies in the Phantoms, no doubt. But that was a point to which I was somewhat indifferent, since they are not supposed to be more than the best human intelligence of their time in a sort of quintessential form. I speak of the 'Years.' The 'Pities' are, of course, merely Humanity with all its weaknesses." March 22, 1904.

In the post-script of a letter to Clodd, February 2, 1908, he added: "The idea of the Unconscious becoming conscious with flux of time is also new, I think, whatever it may be worth. At any rate I have never met with it anywhere. T.H.

19. Quoted in the *Current Literature*, May 1906, pp. 522-3.

20. *The Times Literary Supplement*, February 19, 1920.

21. William R. Rutland, *Thomas Hardy*, p. 334.

22. J. O. Bailey, *Thomas Hardy and the Cosmic Mind* (University of North Carolina Press, Chapel Hill, 1956), p. 188.
   "As servant of the Will, Napoleon is subject to Its reasonless and insatiable hungers, chiefly lust for power and command. Whatever dream the historical Napoleon may have had for Europe ultimately unified, ordered for man's good, and at peace, the Napoleon of *The Dynasts* has no such dream except as a means to his own fame. . . . 'My brain has only one wish—to succeed.'

23. William R. Rutland, p. 335.

24. J. O. Bailey, *Thomas Hardy and the Cosmic Mind* (University of North Carolina Press, 1956), p. 32.

25. Elizabeth C. Hickson, *The Versification of Thomas Hardy* (University of Pennsylvania, 1931), p. 86.

26. Mr. Bailey points out that the Spirit Sinister speaks half his lines in poetry and half in prose: 48 lines in each medium. He said, "I think Hardy found it difficult to express evil in a lyric mood." *Thomas Hardy and the Cosmic Mind* (University of North Carolina Press, Chapel Hill, 1956), p. 77.

27. Edmund Gosse, *Some Diversions of a Man of Letters*, p. 257.

28. William Lyon Phelps, *Essays on Modern English Novelists* (The Macmillan Company, 1910), p. 44.

29. Mrs. Hardy reported this at Max Gate.

30. *T. P.'s Weekly*, December 5, 1914.

31. *The Observer*, September 13, 1925.

32. *The Athenaeum*, November 28, 1914.

33. *The Dynasts*, p. xii, Wessex ed.

34. An unidentified clipping, February 24, 1908, Harvard Theatre Collection.

35. *Daily News*, February 17, 1908.

36. *Ibid.*

37. *Ibid.*

38. Houghton Library, *Notes on The Dynasts* by Thomas Hardy in four letters to Edward Clodd (Edinburgh, printed for private circulation only), 1929.

39. *The Times Literary Supplement*, February 5, 1904.

40. *Current Literature*, May, 1906.

41. *The Times Literary Supplement*, February 16, 1906.

42. Quoted in *Current Literature*, May, 1906, p. 522.

43. *Daily News*, February 17, 1908.

44. *Ibid.*

73

45. Lillah McCarthy, *Myself and My Friends* (London, Thornton Butterworth, Ltd. 1933), p. 102.

46. In the (1903) *Preface,* Hardy said that he had outlined *The Dynasts* about six years back. The year 1897 saw the triumph of Mrs. Fiske as *Tess* in the United States. Did that success influence his choice of medium?

47. Harley Granville Barker was born in London in 1877 and made his first appearance on the stage at Harrogate at the age of fourteen. He toured England with the Ben Greet Players and appeared in *Richard II* with the Elizabethan Stage Society. After touring with Mrs. Patrick Campbell, he became associated with Bernard Shaw in the Incorporated Stage Society and made his name in the production and stage management of Shaw's plays. "With him the stage seemed for once no longer stagey, and what passed there took on, in a surprising and delightful fashion, the complexion of actual life." *The Spectator,* March 20, 1908, p. 499.

   He was also a playwright. Among his works are: *The Marrying of Ann Leete, The Voysey Inheritance,* and with Laurence Housman, *Prunella.*

48. This is the "copy" Miss Irene Cooper Willis entrusted to me after she took it from her book shelf in King's Bench.

49. Max Gate MS.

50. Hardy wrote to William Archer, July 1, 1907: "There is no doubt that Vedrenne-Barker's better sense of true drama than that personated by other London managers is about to be rewarded. I tried to get a place at an afternoon performance at their theatre (Court) last week—at an hour when one can usually reckon with certainty on finding room, but

there was not a seat left in the place I wanted. I hope they may do as well at the Savoy." Archer MS.

51. Max Gate MS (first draft).
52. Max Gate MS.
53. Colby College Collection.
54. Max Gate MS.
55. *The Referee,* interview before the opening, 1914. Harvard Theatre Collection.
56. Carroll A. Wilson MS.
57. Max Gate MS.
58. Mr. Allan Wade, a member of the cast and secretary and assistant, and playreader to Granville Barker (See *Who's Who in the Theatre,* 1939) wrote to me on July 4, 1938, "The whole of 'The Dynasts' was submitted to the Lord Chamberlain for license, and . . . some scenes—not, of course, those played—*were refused a license* (italics mine). Presumably it would not be legally possible in England, to stage the whole work, on a series of nights, could some means of doing so be devised."
59. Unmarked clipping of March 10, 1920. Harvard Theatre Collection.
60. *Public Opinion,* February 5, 1915. This Prologue is also given in the souvenir program of the Toronto performance, February 14, 1916. I am indebted to the late Professor Ernest A. Dale of University College, Toronto, for this program. The Prologue and Epilogue were published by Clement Shorter and inscribed by him as a Christmas card December 23, 1914. The space after the four lines of the second stanza is Shorter's arrangement.
61. The importance of the Reader in *The Dynasts* is indicated in Granville Barker's assignment of the part to so distinguished an actor as Henry Ainley.

This importance is further underlined in conferring on the Reader the honor of speaking such lines as Nelson's unforgettable "England expects . . ." William Archer's discussion of the Reader's role see page 45.

62. Part I, Act VI, Scene iii.

63. This method is known from the Japanese Theatre —also from the Moscow Art Theatre.

64. *The Athenaeum*, November 28, 1914, p. 572.

65. Allan Wade, letter to me, July 4, 1938.

66. *The Spectator*, December 12, 1914.

67. *The Nation*, February 14, 1920.

68. *London World*. (Copied in an unidentified paper December 19, 1914).

69. *The Spectator*, December 12, 1914.

70. Hardy's letter to Charles Morgan, November 14, 1919.

71. *Public Opinion*, February 5, 1915. Also in the Toronto souvenir program. Published by Clement Shorter and inscribed as his Christmas card December 23, 1914.

72. Harris M. Lyon wrote in the *Green Book Magazine* of Archer's criticism of *The Dynasts*: "Dear old William Archer, than whom there is no calmer bonehead in the purlieus of the drama, was there and reported the affair accurately. A careful reading of Will's article shows—honest!—only one mixed metaphor in some two thousand words. He speaks of "fearful wild fowl . . . shedding upon the world-historic spectacle the searchlights of Hardy's pessimistic philosophy!" *Green Book Magazine*, April, 1915.

73. *The Nation* (New York), December 24, 1914, p. 753.

74. *The Referee*, November 29, 1914.

75. *Public Opinion*, February 5, 1915, "Mr. Hardy's Great Triumph."

76. *Ibid.*

77. *The London World* (copied in an unidentified paper, December 19, 1914), Harvard Theatre Collection.

78. "Such stars as Barry Sullivan, Herman Vezin, Edward Compton and Henry Ainley were not only great actors but were great orators as well, each able to carry the weight of a whole play on his own shoulders. Any one of them, when performing a verse play, whether by Shakespeare or another poet, could hold an audience so spellbound that it failed to notice that the supporting company was often anything but first class, or that the scenery was sadly in need of attention of the scenic artist." W. G. Fay, "The Poet and the Actor," *Scattering Branches* (ed. S. L. Gwynn, New York: Macmillan and Company, 1940), p. 119.

79. William Archer, "The Dynasts on the Stage," *The Nation* (New York), December 24, 1914.

80. *Truth* (London), copied in an unidentified paper, dated December 19, 1914. Harvard Theatre Collection.

81. Cf. *The Spectator*, December 12, 1914, p. 840: "Is it possible to combine non-realistic scenery with realistic costumes? It may be denied that illusion is an essential of the theatre, but it must be admitted that *something* was jarred upon by the spectacle of Wellington's staff dressed historically down to the last gaiter-button and standing up against Mr. Norman Wilkinson's purely formal background. Perhaps, with extraordinary skillful lighting, the thing might be achieved. But some of us, at least, are in-

clined to ask for everything or nothing. Either get
a revolving stage and set each scene realistically—
and how, even so, could Waterloo be managed?—
or turn down your lamps, give your characters masks
and Post-Impressionistic clothes, and, in short, treat
The Dynasts frankly as a super puppet-show. The
risks from compromise upon the stage are terrible;
and Mr. Barker's compromise has sometimes brought
him perilously near to a series of *tableaux vivants*
in aid of a deserving charity."

82. Sir Cedric Hardwicke, "The Drama of Tomorrow,"
    The Rede Lecture Cambridge: University Press,
    1936), p. 18.
83. Unidentified, undated, Harvard Theatre Collection.
84. *The Athenaeum*, November 28, 1914.
85. *The Athenaeum*, November 28, 1914.
86. Cf. Allan Wade's letter to me July 4, 1938: "The
    cast took a great interest in the production. Some
    of the parts were very happily cast—for instance,
    Murray Carrington, who played Wellington, had by
    nature almost exactly the features and characteristic
    nose of the Duke. Nicholas Hanner managed to re-
    semble Nelson very closely. On the other hand, the
    late Sydney Valentine, though a very good actor,
    was not physically a convincing Napoleon. There
    was, the program shows, a great deal of 'doubling'
    and those of us who had many changes of uniform
    and make-up were kept very busy."
87. *The Times Literary Supplement*, December 10,
    1914.
88. *Ibid.*
89. *Ibid.*
90. St. John Ervine, *The Theatre in My Time* (London:
    Rich and Cowan Ltd., 1933), p. 148.

91. *The Saturday Review,* March 3, 1900.

92. Florence Emily Hardy, *Life of Hardy,* II, 203-4.

93. Colbourne MS.

94. Colbourne MS.

95. Colbourne MS.

96. *The Observer,* February 8, 1920.

97. Florence Emily Hardy, *Life of Hardy,* II, 204.

98. Maurice Colbourne wrote me, November 22, 1939: "I made the members continue the debate by letter through the vacation, acting myself as a clearing house and pretending to be neutral. Each member was informed of the other members' opinions, answers and counter answers. . . ."

99. Hardy MS.

100. Florence Emily Hardy, *Life of Hardy,* II, 204.

101. Colbourne MS.

102. *The Dynasts,* I, 14-15 (Wessex ed.)

103. *The Dynasts,* III, 255 (Wessex ed.)

104. Max Gate MS.

105. Charles Morgan was the manager of the O. U. D. S. Mrs. Crackenthorpe has used the term "producing" incorrectly. Charles Morgan was in no sense the producer.

106. Max Gate MS.

107. Max Gate MS.

108. This was finally played by Joan, Lady Buckmaster. (Ellen Terry had been previously asked to be one of the Muses.)

109. Max Gate MS.

110. According to *The Times Literary Supplement,* February 2, 1906, Nelson's is "the most famous deathbed in our country."

111. *Christian Science Monitor,* March 9, 1920.

112. *The Observer,* February 15, 1920.

113. *The Times Literary Supplement,* February 19, 1920.
114. *Ibid.*
115. *The Observer,* February 8, 1920.
116. *The Times Literary Supplement,* February 19, 1920.
117. *The Observer,* February 15, 1920.
118. *Christian Science Monitor,* March 9, 1920.
119. *The Times Literary Supplement,* February 19, 1920.
120. *Current History,* May, 1920, p. 644.
121. *The Times Literary Supplement,* February 9, 1920.
122. *The Nation* (New York), March 20, 1920.
123. *Christian Science Monitor,* March 9, 1920.
124. *The Athenaeum,* February 20, 1920.
125. Colbourne MS.
126. Colbourne MS.
127. There was an intermediate production in Toronto the week of February 14, 1916, for the benefit of the Red Cross. It was directed by Frank Lascelles of Oxford, England.
128. *The London Mercury,* October 25, 1925, p. 65.

The Famous Tragedy of the Queen of Cornwall

> Verse plays, it has been generally held,
> should either take their subject matter from
> some mythology or else should be about
> some remote historical period.—T. S. Eliot,
> *Poetry and Drama*

Two years after Granville Barker's production of *The Dynasts* (1916), Hardy began a drama of the opposite *genre*. But not until three years after the Oxford production of *The Dynasts* in 1920 did he resume and finish his one-act play. Then, at the age of eighty-three, Hardy deliberately challenged the attention of the dramatic world whe he published *The Famous Tragedy of the Queen of Cornwall*. In conquering the most rigid of theatrical conventions he must have felt vindicated (for critics had probably made him feel that he needed vindication) for casting his supernatural-historical epic in dramatic form. After the unappreciative early reception of

The Dynasts, one can imagine that Hardy may have delighted in demonstrating that he could write an intense and concentrated tragedy and even observe the unities. At any rate, he illustrated the truth of Goethe's dictum that a good test of genius is to be able to work within limitations: "In der Beschrankung zeigt sich erst der Meister." [1]

Hardy commented on his play in a letter to Mr. Harold Child:

The Unities are strictly preserved, whatever virtrue there may be in that. (I, myself, am old-fashioned enough to think there is a virtue in it, if it can be done without artificiality. The only other case I remember attempting it in was *The Return of the Native.*) The original events could have been enacted in the time taken up by the performance, and they continue unbroken throughout. The change of persons on the stage is called a change of scene, there being no change of background.

My temerity in pulling together into the space of an hour events that in the traditional stories covered a long time will doubtless be criticized, if it is noticed. But there are so many versions of the famous romance that I felt free to adapt it to my purpose in any way—as, in fact, the Greek dramatists did in their plays—notably *Euripides.*

Wishing to be thoroughly English I have dropped the name of Chorus for the conventional onlookers, and call them Chanters, though they play the part of a Greek Chorus to some extent. I have also called them Ghosts (I don't for the moment recall an instance of this in a Greek play).

. . . Whether the lady ghosts in our performance will submit to have their faces whitened I don't know! . . .

I have tried to avoid turning the rude personages of, say, the fifth century into respectable Victorians, as was done by Tennyson, Swinburne, Arnold, etc. On the other hand it would have been impossible to present them as they really were, with their barbaric manners and surroundings.[2]

In the pathetic story of Tristram and Iseult, Hardy found dramatic material that particularly suited his genius. From medieval times innumerable writers have been inspired by the tragical amours of Tristram. Chretien de Troyes, Marie de France, Beroul, the Anglo-Norman Thomas, de Saint More, Gilbert and Gottfried of Strassburg, as well as Malory were among the early tellers of the tale of the "irresistible and fatal force of love,"[3] of which modern poets have been no less fond. As Tennyson, Matthew Arnold, and Swinburne retold the famous romance before Hardy, so have Robinson, Masefield, and John Erskine after him. While it is beyond the limits of this study to discuss the old legend in its various versions, the following comparison is interesting. Massingham says:

Tennyson . . . turns Tristram into a Knight of the Victorian order, sensual and sentimental. Hardy, with his deeper and simpler human feeling, keeps him primitive and strong. The effect of this simplicity is not to weaken the pathos of the drama, but to enhance it. The more direct the dealing with the human stuff of the play, the more homely the pattern of blank verse, the greater the dramatic possibilities proved to be.[4]

In the emotional conflicts of the two enamoured Iseults, in the clash of the crabbed King Mark with the ardent Sir Tristram, and in their struggle with the whims of Fate and the fatality of love, we recognize characteristics of Hardy's poetry and prose. For as Massingham has pointed out "Hardy is of all poets, new and old, the lover and the mourner of the ill-mated. His Iseult of Cornwall comes of a long line of predecessors. She is Eustacia Vye. She is Sergeant Troy. She is 'The History of the Hardcomes.' " [5]

With exquisite simplicity and homely beauty Hardy tells the destruction of the doom-begotten lovers. In the manner of the Greek dramatists and of Ibsen, he begins just before the catastrophe—literally in the last hour. Through the chanters [6] and through the retrospection of the main characters we learn that while King Mark has been absent from Lyonnesse on a hunting expedition Iseult was summoned to Brittany by Tristram, her dying lover. She did not land, however, because Iseult of the White Hands met her at the shore and falsely informed her of the death of Tristram.

As the Queen lands on Cornish soil before King Mark returns from the chase, she thinks that she is providentially spared his suspicions and enquiries. But as the curtain rises we find that King Mark has been slyly informed of his Queen's actions:

That while I've sued the chase you followed him,
Vanishing on a voyage of some days,
Which you'd fain cloak from me, and have confessed
To no one, either, of my people here.

The Queen tells of Tristram's death, but King Mark doubts its truth:

He has died too many many times for that report
to hold!

The Queen muses on the King's words:

How little he knows, does Mark! And yet how much?
Can there be any groundage for his thought
That Tristram's not a ghost? Oh, no such hope!

Immediately after Iseult explains to Brangwain the
purpose and issue of her trip to Brittany, admitting that
she had even thought of bringing White-Hands, Tristram's wife, along to Cornwall with Tristram, a messenger
arrives with the news that Tristram is recovered and is
on his way to Cornwall. Mark is in bibulous council with
his knights when Tristram arrives disguised as a minstrel.
Tristram and Iseult discuss Tristram's wretched marriage
to King Howel's daughter, whom he received as recom-
pense for having saved her father's lands. The scene ends
with Tristram's beautiful love song, "Let's meet again
tonight, my Fair."

A strange ship arrives on the Cornish shore bringing
Tristram's wife, Iseult of the White Hands. She confesses
to Tristram that she sent the Queen of Cornwall away
from Brittany, but she pleads her love. While Queen Iseult
overhears, Tristram upbraids White-Hands and tries to
induce her to go back to Brittany.

Then Hardy makes his original contribution to the
old legend in causing the two Iseults to meet in the castle
of Lyonnesse. During the interview, White-Hands faints
and is carried off by Tristram and Brangwain. When she
recovers, the Queen orders her placed in her own bed.
"The tragedy of ill-matched mates can have no solution,
for Mark is mean, Tristram is weak, and the two women

are lost in love for him." [7] King Mark overhears the Queen and Tristram. Tristram is warned by a damsel to beware of Mark. She brings a letter for Mark which Tristram does not read. Iseult begs him to save himself and forget her. He refuses. Then both have forebodings of death. Tristram sings of sadness. Iseult weeps. Tristram embraces her, and King Mark creeps up behind with a glittering dagger and (against all the rules of chivalry) stabs him in the back. Tristram turns on Mark and says in death:

> From you!—against whom never have I sinned
> But under sorcery unwittingly,
> By draining deep the love-compelling vial
> In my sick thirst, as innocently did she! . . .

Queen Iseult snatches Mark's dagger and stabs Mark. Then taking Tristram's brachet with her, she leaps over the ledge into the sea.

Mr. Massingham has pointed out that it is the meeting of the two Iseults which imprints Hardy's plastic touch and inimitable seal on the legend. "The humble wife and the proud mistress must meet, or the play would have been a commonplace murder. As it was, it closed on a soul-encounter as stirring as Macbeth's duel with Macduff. . . . But the discovery in the Hardy play is not of its charm but of its intensity." [8]

An article in *The Times Literary Supplement* says:

> Hardy has told the story, as all would expect of him, with a fine strictness of outline, enclosing intense emotion; and, as usual when a master takes up a well-known story, he will be found to have left his mark upon it. The story of Tristram and Iseult

has been called a poor story, and it has been called the greatest love story in the world. Some of those who were unable to let it alone have tried to brush and comb it and make it a little more presentable than they found it. Others have gone to the opposite extreme and have used it to glorify illicit love. Between the two there still rests the story itself; and it is in the story itself neither prettified nor brutalized, but firmly and finely told, that we hear from Mr. Hardy.

Perhaps it is his long brooding over the tale which has found a voice in the distinguishing quality of this play's sentiment, which we take to be a manly pity. It is not Mr. Hardy's way to blame, or to excuse. It is his way to show the conditions as he sees them, and to bid us think what else could have happened but what did happen. The story of Tristram and Iseult shares this with some Greek tragic tales—that besides compulsion of character there is compulsion of fate. We cannot escape from the story because, if we declare that these lovers were weak and wicked, we are answered by Brangwain and the love-potion. Fate willed; and therefore we are free to pity with whole heart. It was sad and mad and bad; but they could not help it. . . . If Mark had died and Tristram had never married! If anything could have happened to stay the course of destiny! But the truth was not pleasant, and it must be told.[9]

To complete the story, to explain what led up to the situation and to comment on the action, as we noted in Hardy's letter, he gives his story something like a chorus of an old Greek tragedy: the shades of dead old Cornish-

87

men and of dead old Cornish women. The women chanters cry when the tragedy is complete:

> This is no falsehood fell,
> But very truth indeed
> That we too surely read!
> Would that we had to tell
> But pleasant truth alway!

Mr. Rutland Boughton says in "A Musical Association
with Thomas Hardy" that Hardy not only wrote the script
of this play for the Hardy Players but in at least one instance consciously suited a role to an individual actor.
Hardy added the prologue and epilogue for the character
of Merlin, Mr. Boughton says, "for no artistic reason, but
because without it one of the Hardy Players (for whom
the play was originally written) would have been without
a part." [10] Just as in 1914 Hardy elaborated the role of
the waiting-maid in *Wessex Scenes from The Dynasts* so
that Dorchester's leading lady, Gertrude Bugler, would
have a part, so we find in 1923 Hardy added the character
of Merlin, so that Mr. Tilley, veteran actor, stage manager, and writer for the Hardy Players, would not be
omitted from the cast. Hardy could not have shown more
plainly that *The Famous Tragedy of the Queen of Cornwall* belonged to the Hardy Players than by allowing them
to produce it in Dorchester just thirteen days after its
publication. A critic of their later production in King
George's Hall says, "As he has always done, Thomas
Hardy insists that these simple-hearted Wessex townsfolk
are the people to whom he and his play belong, and only
out of such performances that a truly racial drama can
grow." [11]

But Hardy did not content himself merely with writing a play suitable for the 1923 program of the Hardy Players. As Hannen Swaffer says, "To such an extent does Mr. Hardy take charge of performances that, although he is eighty-three, he goes to the length of revising the program, sub-editing its wording, adding necessary notes, and is as keenly interested as his friend, Barrie, in his own productions." [12] Perhaps the supreme expression of Hardy's interest in his play is shown by his inviting Sir James Barrie and Harley Granville Barker down to Dorchester to attend a rehearsal three weeks before the performance. This was a unique occasion for the village cast. To perform the finished play, *Tess,* before Hardy at Max Gate was an exciting experience for the professional Garrick cast from London, but to have Hardy and two of the most distinguished and expert dramatists and directors of England at a rehearsal must have been almost overwhelming for village players. But by 1923 the Hardy Players were accustomed to celebrities. Their rehearsal impressed the two dramatic experts in different manners. Barrie was most enthusiastic. He told Mr. Tilley that never before had he seen a cast, professional or amateur, which was word perfect three weeks before their performance. Granville Barker, on the contrary, saw room for improvement and wrote Mr. Tilley, the stage manager, a long letter giving detailed suggestions for word and line.[13] He added, however, that his suggestions might be found impractical for amateur use. Both Mrs. Hardy and Mr. Tilley told me that his suggestions were not incorporated in the scheme of production. Perhaps they came too late, but more probably they were beyond the amateurs. At any rate, Hardy was interested enough to keep Granville Barker's letter to the manager; and it was probably because of this discussion of such technical matters which caused Mrs. Hardy to record that "the performance, and particularly the rehearsals, gave Hardy considerable pleasure." [14]

The Famous Tragedy of the Queen of Cornwall is unique in Hardy's dramatic writing in that it is the only drama within stage limitations which he wrote originally for actors and which he also considered worthy of publication. It will be remembered that it differed from *The Mumming Play of Saint George* which was first incorporated in *The Return of the Native* and from *The Three Wayfarers* which was originally *The Three Strangers* of the *Wessex Tales*. Hardy wrote *O Jan! O Jan! O Jan!* also for the Hardy Players but for some reason he did not publish it; nor did he publish *Wessex Scenes from The Dynasts,* bits culled from his gigantic masterpiece for production in aid of the Red Cross during the war. So it is, therefore, significant that at the age of eighty-three Hardy not only wrote a drama—a drama for actors within theatrical limitations—but one which was also in his opinion literature. Thirty-one years after writing "Why I Don't Write Plays," Hardy gave Dorchester and the English reading public *The Famous Tragedy of the Queen of Cornwall.*

As the Hardy Players presented the drama just thirteen days after the publication of *The Queen of Cornwall* I am not sure whether their version is earlier or later than the printed one. There are a few variations which seem to have been made while the play was in production. And the following statement of Mr. Boughton's shows that Hardy made some changes after sending his work to the press: "He accepted all my suggestions for the music drama, and copied into my volume of *The Queen* those passages which he added subsequent to its first publication. . . ." If we judge from the interest Hardy took in the Dorchester production, we may conclude that he

revised his script to meet the theatrical needs. But since
the differences in the two versions are so slight (as I find
in comparing Mr. Tilley's prompt copy with the first
edition), the question of priority is of no great importance.
Yet it is very significant of Hardy's interest in the Hardy
Players, that he added a four-line stanza to one of Tristram's songs for their production, while a year later,
when Mr. Boughton wanted some lyrics for his opera to
relieve the emotion, "to prevent the feeling from becoming intolerable," he could not persuade Hardy to write a
line.

Most of the changes in the acting version were in the
omission of lines from Queen Iseult's speeches, especially
the asides with no dramatic value, for example, in Scene
XIV, the Queen's comment on the arrival of White Hands
is cut:

> Not my suspicion hardneed into mould
> Of flesh and blood indeed?

and the line following

> She has no claim to importune like that,

which is,

> And gloss her hardihood in tracking him!

Another aside which is cut is:

> I can't stand this!

One wonders if it were not on the advice of Barrie or
Granville Barker that Hardy abandoned the outworn

asides. Perhaps, too, at their suggestion the lines of the chanters were sometimes broken up for individual actors.

In Scene XV the following speech is divided between three chanters:

> White Hands did this,
> Desperate to win again
>
> Back to her kiss
> One she would miss!—
>
> Yea, from the Queen again
> Win for her bliss!

There are several places where Hardy has changed a single word, or phrase, or line:

In Scene XIV, the published line is:

> I for a *leastness* longer could abide

which corresponds in the acting version to

> I for a *leastwhile* longer could abide.

Scene XIV also has

> I'd fade your face to strangeness *in my eyes*

while the prompt copy reads

> I'd fade your face to strangeness *unto mine!*

The two most interesting variations in the poetry are

found in the songs of Tristram. The first stanza of his loveliest love lyric appears in the text:

> Let's meet again to-night, my Fair,
> Let's meet unseen of all;
> The day-god labours to his lair,
> And then the even fall! [15]

The third line in the Players' version is

> The daylight drifts like gossamere.

If Hardy substituted this beautiful lyrical line for "The day-god labours in his lair," he did it for its charm, but in doing so he sacrificed dramatic power. Tristram's impatience in waiting for a tryst with Iseult is more excellently expressed by the *labouring* of the day-god than by the *drifting* of gossamere. But whether Tristram in a lyric should express dramatic feeling or lovely poetic images we shall not debate. It is likely that the printed version is later, since Mr. Boughton also uses it.

The stanza that Hardy added to Tristram's last song is valuable dramatically. After White Hand's arrival in Cornwall, and Mark's disposition is known, Tristram with good reason sings to Iseult:

> Yes, Love, true is it sadness suits me best!
> Sad, sad we are; sad, sad shall ever be.
> What shall deliver us from Love's unrest,
> And bonds we did not forecast, did not see!

The dramatic irony of the words is excellent when we know that Mark is about ready to deliver him "from Love's unrest." But to heighten that crisis Hardy elaborates Tristram's forebodings in an additional unpublished stanza:

If, Love, the night fall on us, dark of hope
Let us be true, whatever else may be
Let us be strong, and without wavering cope
With unjust Dooms, though such we did not see.[16]

The stage direction of the acting version has Mark with a glittering dagger creep up behind Tristram who is embracing Iseult. And it is a question of seconds before Tristram meets his unjust Doom which he did not foresee. Then Iseult stabs Mark and jumps over the cliff with Tristram's hound, Houdain.

The Dorchester Players presented *The Queen of Cornwall* in "a pleasant hearty way." Mrs. Hardy records, "The great difficulties which the play presented to amateur actors, unaccustomed to reciting blank verse, who were at their best in rustic comedy, were more or less overcome. . . ." [17] A cable to New York said, "The local color was amazing. One had not realized that King Mark of Cornwall and his subjects spoke with the broad west country accent, but they probably did; and in this respect the performance was amazingly alive." [18]

Massingham praised the acting of Miss Fare:

It happened that the lady who played the Princess of Brittany was as near an actress of genius as one can look for in a company of zealous amateurs in a country town. Had her fellow of Cornwall been of the same rare metal, they would indeed have made an electric affair of it.[19]

As it was, Edmund Gosse wrote, "His play is a wonderful

performance." [20] And a special cable to the *New York Herald,* November 29, 1923, said, "critics said that in *The Queen of Cornwall* Hardy proved he could have been a great dramatist." [21]

As it happened with the six earlier productions that were taken to London, the criticisms there were more severe, but even in London critics saw the appropriateness of Hardy's play in the hands of the West Country players. One critic observed:

> It is obvious that this beautiful little folk-tragedy was, technically speaking, dropped completely. From the commonplace theatrical standpoint Miss Fare, as Iseult of the White Hands—true Dorchester and very good indeed—was the only Hardy Player who got near to tragic expression. But if one looked at the whole affair in the spirit of the best of playgoers, Duke Theseus, how much one could find that was beautiful and memorable. . . . Of course, I should like to see *The Queen of Cornwall* perfectly done. Failing that, give me this. Alderman Tilley's Merlin, for instance—how much more truly the words came in the broad, unaffected Dorset speech than from some alien elocutionist! How infinitely more point in the assertion, which Hardy makes through Merlin himself, that those "warriors and ladies dead" were our neighbors and "like ourselves." [22]

Mrs. Hardy refers to the London performance as "not altogether a success, partly owing to the only building available having no stage suitable for the performance, a rather small concert platform having to be used." [23]

After the production by the Hardy Players there were

many requests for *The Queen of Cornwall*. Even in October, 1923, before the Dorchester production, the Pegasus Film Company asked to make a moving picture of the amateurs in it, but Hardy felt that their performance was not far enough along at that time to grant this request. Epsom College in Surrey was granted permission to perform it, but I find no record of its production there. In February, 1924, Margaret Anglin asked Hardy for the privilege of presenting *The Queen of Cornwall*, but I have no evidence of her doing so. The Royal Academy of Dramatic Art in London gave a performance which caused Hardy much worry. On April 11, 1924, Mrs. Hardy wrote to Sir Sydney Cockerell:

> Some man, without asking permission, has set part of *The Queen of Cornwall* to music, and it was performed by students of some Dramatic Academy, without our knowledge. Naturally poor Rutland Boughton, who had been spending weeks in composing music, imagining that he was to be the sole composer, was perturbed and wrote for an explanation. T. H. was nearly driven frantic and said he could not stand the worry—etc., etc. I implored him to put his affairs into the hands of yourself, or one of the Macmillans, or someone whom he likes and trusts. But it was of no use. Fortunately, after a couple of days, he calmed down.[24]

This performance, however, was said by *The Daily Telegraph* to be "all our imagination painted it." [25] The Radcliffe Idler gave *The Queen of Cornwall* for a spring pageant on the Agassiz steps, May 16, 1926. And it is interesting to note that about two years before Masefield pub-

96

lished his *Tristan and Isolt,* Hardy's play was given in his music room, at Hill Crest, Boars Hill, on a program with T. Sturge More's *Medea.*[26] But the most important presentation of *The Queen of Cornwall* was that of Mr. Rutland Boughton.

According to Mr. J. O. Strong, Mr. Boughton studied composition under Charles Villiers Stanford, Professor of Composition and Director of Opera and Orchestra at the Royal College of Music, along with Vaughan-Williams, Holst, Dunhill, Gatty, and Coleridge Taylor. After discussing Holst and Vaughan-Williams, Mr. Strong says:

A third pupil, Rutland Boughton, almost requires a separate article for full treatment; firstly, because he is the one English composer who has relied exclusively on the dramatic form for his substantial works, and secondly, because he early forsook the hope of performance in the ordinary way, and he took steps to produce his own works, all of which have been given their first performance. Starting in 1913 at Glastonbury in Somerset with a small band of devoted adherents, he had by 1926 given some 300 performances of his own and other operas and plays. Almost throughout he was his own producer, chorus master, conductor and— through the medium of the piano—his own orchestra.[27]

It was my privilege to be invited by Rutland Boughton to come over from Dorchester to Bath to talk to him during that busy week preceding the premiere of *The Ever Young,* in September 1935. In the Pavilion Theatre during one of the final rehearsals Mr. Boughton told me how he happened to make an opera of *The Queen of Cornwall*. As he has given a full account in "A Musical Association with Thomas Hardy," I shall quote from it:

The first I heard of *The Queen of Cornwall* was in a review by a daily paper. The reviewer was of the opinion that the play was the production of a senile artist. But, fortunately, I chanced to see also the review in *The Daily Telegraph*, and that not only spoke fairly of the play but quoted some of its lines. Those lines made it clear enough that it was the other man, not Hardy, who was senile— young and modern though the reviewer was believed to be. . . .

Having read the *Telegraph* notice, I toured the booksellers of London, and at last got a copy of the first edition—a copy which the shopkeeper had put by for himself. And in an A.B.C. near by the mood was evoked which, if encouraged, meant music sooner or later. Two days later Herbert Lambert posted to me another copy, with a note asking if it were not the very thing for Glastonbury, where we had made a persistent stand for choral drama. The only difficulty, so far as I was concerned, lay in the unrelieved grimness of the tragedy. The swift pain of the spoken work found relief enough in the exquisite songs which Hardy had given to Tristram, but when set to music the emotional expression of the bulk of the work would be doubled, and those two songs would not be nearly enough to prevent the feeling from becoming intolerable. It was not a question of making the work palatable for superficial tastes, but the actual weakness which would result from continuously playing on a single series of emotions. My study of the Alkestis of Euripides had shown me with what amazing intuition the Greek dramatist had carried each section of his work to its separate climax, and then relieved it and prepared our emotions for the next section by a chorus which, while remaining entirely apropos, lifted the weight of tragedy into the less personal and the nobler realm of mass emotion. (For, contrary to general belief, mass emotion is a very noble thing when the individuals of the mass are engaged in an impersonal service.) But what had been possible in the drama of Euripides was impossible in this play of Hardy's wherein the chorus themselves are but ghosts of the common men and women he had taught us to love and to pity in his tales—ghosts, moreover, who are intent on emphasizing and not at all on relieving the pain of the story. The only chance of making the play right for musical expression depended on the willingness of the author to reconsider it afresh from a point of view which he could scarcely be expected to appreciate, or on the existence of lyrics of his own which would exactly fit, verbally and emotionally, into those places where they were needed. An unlikely thing, but it happened all the same. I read again his poems from cover to cover, and discovered six poems which might have been written for *The Queen of Cornwall* itself. So I approached Hardy, asked if I might make a musical version of the play, if he would be willing for the extra lyrics to be interpolated, and for certain cuts to be made in the existing text. He suggested that I should call and consult him; and, of course, he proved to be the generous and friendly artist one would have expected from the simple quality of his work. He accepted all my suggestions for the music-drama, and copied into my volume of *The Queen* those passages which he added subsequent to its first publication, in case they might be found suitable for the musical version also.[28]

Mr. Boughton told me also that Hardy's play was already modeled to music with its choruses (as *The Dynasts* is with the strophe and antistrophe) and thus needed very little modification. Mr. Boughton preferred to cut the prologue and the epilogue, and in the place of the latter he substituted Hardy's lyric, "A Spot," sung by the Chorus of Shades at the end of the work. He included five other lyrics from Hardy's collected poems in order to develop the emotion as one always does in setting a piece to music. They were: "Bereft she thinks she dreams," "When I set out for Lyonnesse," "The End of the Episode," "If it's ever Spring again," and "Beeny Cliff." When Mr. Boughton on June 11, 1924 went down to Max Gate and suggested these interpolations, Hardy admitted that the lyrics seemed to have been written for the opera. What could be more appropriate, for instance, than to have Tristram, disguised as a harper, sing on his return to Cornwall "When I Set Out for Lyonnesse"? Or for Tristram and Iseult to sing to each other, "O, the opal and the sapphire of that wandering western sea" from "Beeny Cliff"? Or even for Iseult the Whitehanded to sing after King Mark has stabbed her husband

Indulge no more may we
In this sweet-bitter pastime:
The love-light shines the last time
Between you, Dear, and me.[29]

100

and before falling over Tristram's body

> Smile out; but stilly suffer:
> The paths of love are rougher
> Than thoroughfares of stones.[30]

And just as fittingly do the chanters sing the last chorus for the epilogue:

> In years defaced and lost
> Two sat here transport-tossed
> Lit by a living love
> The wilted world knew nothing of:[31]

Hardy was naturally much interested in Boughton's ideas and music, although as Mrs. Hardy records, "he had heard no modern compositions, not even the immensely popular 'Faerie Song' from *The Immortal Hour*.[32] Mr. Tilley told me that he was invited to Max Gate during Boughton's visit to hear him play some of his music, but Mr. Tilley admitted that he knew nothing about music and consequently could not judge it. Hardy, on the contrary, was greatly impressed, and after the composer left, he said—so Mrs. Hardy told me—"If there ever has been a genius in this house, it is Rutland Boughton."

One can easily see why Rutland Boughton would appeal to Hardy. They were both interested in developing a native racial art. For fifteen years Hardy had encouraged the Hardy Players in Dorchester. For ten years Boughton had been working in Glastonbury and Malvern trying to develop a national opera. Boughton's object in founding his festivals was to establish a school of music-drama in which the national consciousness should have full expression, and in which the larger emotional problems affecting his countrymen should be dealt with in terms of symbols familiar to the English people. Thus, many of his works are dramatizations of English or early British myths. One of his Arthurian music-dramas, *The Round Table,* has peace as its main theme.[33] And in the old saga of the love of Tristram and Iseult, Hardy and Boughton found ideal British material for the art of both. "Nationalism in art, properly interested," says Mr. Strong, "is the best sort of nationalism, and, indeed is necessary to the continuance of the health of the artistic part of the activity of a community, and that is an important part of civilization." [34]

Writing of Boughton's philosophy of art in an article, "The Tragedy of the Ill-Matched Pair," Stuart Fletcher says:

> It might be thought that by applying himself to a form of music which has hitherto received scant consideration, Boughton has been deliberately walking out into the desert. It may yet prove, however, that he has discovered and cultivated an oasis, and that it is the desert which he has left behind him.
>
> Listeners to *The Queen of Cornwall* will find that the work teems with ravishing tunes and that though there are passages of a harshness inseparable from such a tragic theme, there is none of the empty-hearted clatter and cheapjack sensationalism to which so much of modern music is prone. The sort of music that Boughton writes can probably be best indicated by one of his favorite sayings. "Music should serve," he says, "for life is more important than art." [35]

The Queen of Cornwall was given at Glastonbury, Malvern, Bournemouth, and Bath. Hardy went to see the opera at Glastonbury in 1924, and again to Bournemouth for the new orchestral arrangement by Sir Dan Godfrey. His reactions are recorded by Rutland Boughton:

> On each occasion his few criticisms were much to the point and never captious. Just as he had accepted Baron d'Erlanger's operatic setting, and an American film version of *Tess,* as things outside his sphere, so where the music and the orchestra were concerned he left *The Queen* to my honour as an artist to do my best. On those points where our arts touched his judgments were what anyone would have wished—directed only to the future betterment of the production. When the musical version seemed to bring off a detail that was worth while—as in the swift nature of a climax, he was instant in his recognition and approval. Indeed, I think it may well be recognized by now that Hardy was something much greater than an artist.[36]

One interesting observation that Hardy made at Glastonbury after the opera, so Boughton told me, was that in the play the sympathies of the audience were with White Hands, while in the opera the sympathies are with the Queen of Cornwall. By inserting the lyrics, the composer gives the Queen a fuller expression of her love for Tristram and her helplessness in the hands of Fate, so that the audience is inclined to condone her actions and pity her. The character of Tristram also seems to be changed in its musical setting. Stuart Fletcher said:

> Tristram is the typical Romantic artist. He is not

unlike Dubedat in Shaw's Doctor's Dilemna. He has beautiful things to give (his songs are the loveliest things in the work) and claims in return the right to be irresponsible. Whenever a crisis requiring a decision occurs in his affairs, he postpones the difficulty with a song. In one of these songs, "Foreboding," he sings optimistically of the future, but the music of the song reveals his fundamental despondence. This use of the music to reveal the falsehood of the word actually spoken is the essence of Music-drama.[37]

On January 13, 14, 14, 1927, the Liverpool Repertory Opera gave *The Queen of Cornwall* at the David Lewis Theatre. The playbill contained this announcement:

The production—the outstanding one of the Liverpool Opera's third season—will be the occasion of the personal visit of Mr. Boughton on the opening night. The orchestra will be augmented for the three evenings, and the entire production should repeat the earlier triumph of the same composer's *Immortal Hour,* who here has Thomas Hardy, the doyen of our poets and novelists as collaborator.[38]

On February 1, 1935, a special version of *The Queen of Cornwall* was broadcast on the B.B.C. It was arranged by Rutland Boughton and directed by Mr. Albert Coates. Whether *The Queen of Cornwall* in its operatic or orchestral arrangements will live is doubtful. Whether professional and amateur actors will continue to demand Hardy's play is a matter of conjecture; yet if it is never produced again, it has proved to be a strong actable drama. Truly *The Queen of Cornwall*—even more than *The Dynasts*—illustrated the fact that Hardy might have conquered the technique of the commercial stage and have become an expert professional dramatist—especially if he had started before the age of eighty-three. At any rate, this short poetic drama with its original treatment of a well-worn theme, with its vivid characterization, its swift action, and flexible blank verse, makes one feel that Hardy made a contribution at last in the field of his first aspiration, the poetic drama. In viewing the mistakes in craftsmanship, one is reminded of Sibelius's remark about Brahms, "Everything written by a genius is interesting, whatever his aesthetic ideas may be, and in spite of all his mistakes and imperfections." [39]

Conclusion

Although Hardy's response to the stage wavered at different times in his career, his attraction to the poetic drama appears consistent and strong throughout his long life. It is true that he turned away from his first aspiration in writing poetic drama in 1867 because of the stage realities and the advice of the manager of the Haymarket; yet the desire within him was strong enough at that time, so that he would have been willing to spend six months learning the technique of the stage. Frustrated at this crucial moment, Hardy put away the idea of writing poetic drama for almost thirty years.

With the prose drama, on the other hand, the pressure invariably came from the outside, from the theatrical world of critics, producers, actors, and actresses. The staging of *Far from the Madding Crowd* in 1882 came from the initiative of J. Comyns Carr, who dramatized the novel; just as that for *The Mayor of Casterbridge* came years later from John Drinkwater. Hardy's own dramatization of *The Three Strangers* in 1893 followed a request of his friend, Barrie. His own dramatic version of *Tess of the D'Urbervilles* followed only tardily after requests from such producers as George Alexander of the St. James's Theatre and the imploring letters from actresses such as Eleanor Duse, Sarah Bernhardt, Ellen Terry, Mrs. Patrick Campbell, and Olga Nethersole.

In April, 1891, even while Hardy was putting the finishing touches on *Tess of the D'Urbervilles,* he was thinking of "a drama of the first Napoleon." Although he does not say in his diary that he was contemplating the work to be in poetic drama, yet years later after the first volume appeared, he expressed the opinion in the *Times* that this was the *only* way to treat the subject. In the years following the critical assault on *Tess,* which appeared in 1891, and later on *Jude* in 1895, Hardy turned his back forever on prose fiction and chose for the medium of his monumental masterpiece his early love, the poetic drama.

He says in the *Preface* to *The Dynasts* that nothing interfered with the writing of his epic drama. Likewise we have noted nothing interfered with the productions of *The Dynasts.* Although many unusual things hindered the various productions of *Tess* in its film, operatic, and stage versions, such as the result of the death of sovereigns, the eruption of Vesuvius and the strike of musicians at Milan, not even war kept Granville Barker's version of *The Dynasts* from materializing at the Kingsway. In fact, it was because of the war that *The Dynasts* was staged in London and Oxford.

Hardy obviously enjoyed his association with Barker,

Colbourne, and Morgan in the years 1914 and 1920 just as he had enjoyed the annual tribute of his fellow townsmen in Dorchester from 1908 to 1924 in their seventy-two performances of fourteen plays based on his work. For them at the age of eighty-three he wrote his final work, *The Famous Tragedy of The Queen of Cornwall*—a one-act poetic drama. His musical association with Rutland Boughton and his attendance at the Glastonbury and Bournemouth productions of the opera, *The Queen of Cornwall,* must have added interest to his declining years.

When I asked Mrs. Hardy if Hardy enjoyed having his work on the stage she said, "He loved it." No doubt he shared Lawrence Housman's feeling expressed in *The Unexpected Years*: "In my experience, the production of plays can provide an author with livelier satisfaction than the writing of books. It is pleasant to be told that one's books are appreciated; but it is not merely pleasant, it is thrilling to see one's play or its characters brought to life by good production or good acting." [40]

Notes on The Famous Tragedy of the Queen of Cornwall

1. Johann Wolfgang von Goethe, "Natur und Kunst" *Die Lese der deutchen Lyrik,* edited by Friedrich Bruns (New York, F. S. Crofts, 1938), p. 122.
2. Florence Emily Hardy, *Life of Hardy,* II, 235-6.
3. Edmund Gosse, *Sunday Times and Sunday Special,* November 18, 1923.
4. H. W. Massingham, *T.P. and Cassell's Weekly,* December 22, 1923.
5. *Ibid.*
6. " 'The Chanters,' both men and women, are employed by Mr. Hardy to give the pitiful aspect to Fate: even Merlin who speaks Prologue and Epilogue of the drama, is on the side of the angels." *Boston Herald,* December 9, 1928.
7. *The Radio Times,* January 25, 1935.
8. W. H. Massingham, *T.P. and Cassell's Weekly,* December 22, 1923.
9. *The Times Literary Supplement,* November 15, 1923.
10. Rutland Boughton, "A Musical Association with

Thomas Hardy," *Musical News and Herald,* February, 1928.

11. *The Referee,* February 24, 1924.

12. Unidentified clipping, "Plays and Playgoers," November 18, 1923.

13. Max Gate MS.

14. Florence Emily Hardy, *Life of Hardy,* II, p. 236.

15. This lyric could be compared with the *serena* of the troubadours, for "in the *serena* the lover longs for the approach of evening, which is to unite him with his beloved." H. J. Chaytor, *The Troubadours* (Cambridge: University Press, 1912), pp. 33-34.

16. Tilley MS.

17. Florence Emily Hardy, *Life of Hardy,* II, 236.

18. *New York Herald,* November 29, 1923.

19. *T.P.* and *Cassell's Weekly,* December 22, 1923.

20. *Sunday Times and Sunday Special,* November 18, 1923.

21. *New York Herald,* November 29, 1923.

22. *The Referee,* February 24, 1924.

23. Florence Emily Hardy, *Life of Hardy,* II, 237.

24. *Friends of a Lifetime* (Jonathan Cape, London, 1940), p. 310.

25. *The Daily Telegraph,* Undated, Harvard Theatre Collection.

26. Mr. Masefield said that *The Queen of Cornwall* was given January 1, 2, 3, 1925. Letter to me April 1, 1937.

27. J. O. Strong, "English Opera since Sullivan," *Theatre Arts Monthly,* August, 1935.

28. Rutland Boughton, "A Musical Association with Thomas Hardy," *Musical News and Herald,* 1928, p. 33.

29. "The End of the Episode," *Collected Poems of*

Thomas Hardy, Macmillan and Co. Ltd. (London, 1932), p. 211.

30. *Ibid.*
31. "A Spot," *Collected Poems,* p. 127.
32. Florence Emily Hardy, *Life of Hardy,* II, 237.
33. *The Radio Times,* January 25, 1935. Under *Notable Music for the Week.*
34. *Theatre Arts Monthly,* "English Opera since Sullivan," August, 1935.
35. *The Radio Times,* January 25, 1935.
36. Rutland Boughton, "A Musical Association with Thomas Hardy," *Musical News and Herald,* February, 1928, p. 34.
37. *The Radio Times,* January 25, 1935.
38. Roberts MS.
39. Bengt de Torne, *Sibelius: A Close-up* (London: Faber and Faber, 1937), p. 62.

Conclusion

40. Lawrence Housman, *The Unexpected Years* (Indianapolis, Bobbs-Merrill Co., 1936), p. 205.